RICHIE ASHBURN'S
PHILLIES TRIVIA

By Richie Ashburn with Allen Lewis

RUNNING PRESS
Philadelphia, Pennsylvania

Copyright © 1983 by Running Press
All rights reserved under the Pan-American
and International Copyright Conventions.
Printed in the United States of America.

Canadian representative: John Wiley & Sons Canada, Ltd.
22 Worcester Road, Rexdale, Ontario M9W 1L1
International representatives: Kaiman & Polon, Inc.
2175 Lemoine Avenue, Fort Lee, New Jersey 07024

9   8   7   6   5   4   3   2
Digit on the right indicates the number of this printing.

Library of Congress Cataloging in Publication Data
Ashburn, Richie.
Richie Ashburn's Phillies trivia.
Includes index.
Summary: More than 300 questions and answers
presenting little-known facts about the
Philadelphia Phillies.
1. Philadelphia Phillies (Baseball team)—Miscellanea
—Juvenile literature. [1. Philadelphia Phillies
(Baseball team)—Miscellanea. 2. Baseball—Miscellanea.
3. Questions and answers.] I. Title. II. Title:
Phillies trivia.
GV875.P45A83   1983   796.357'64'0974811   83-3335

ISBN 0-89471-219-5 (paperback)
ISBN 0-89471-220-9 (library binding)

Logo on cover Registered® Service Mark
licensed by The Phillies.
Cover design by Toby Schmidt
Cover photograph and interior photographs
courtesy of
the Philadelphia Phillies
Baseball cards courtesy of
Mid-Atlantic Coin Exchange, Swarthmore, PA
Typography: Korinna by CompArt, Philadelphia, PA
Printed by Port City Press, Baltimore, MD

This book may be ordered from the publisher. Please
include 75¢ postage. **But try your bookstore first.**

Running Press
125 South 22nd Street
Philadelphia, Pennsylvania 19103

1 Q. *Which teams opposed each other in the first National League game ever played?*

A. Philadelphia and Boston. On April 22, 1876, Boston beat Philadelphia, 6 to 5, before 3,000 fans at 29th Street and Jefferson Avenue, Philadelphia. That Philadelphia team, known as the Athletics, did not complete that season, and the city was not again represented in the National League until the Phillies came into being in 1883. The first game played by the Phillies was on May 1, 1883, at Philadelphia's Recreation Park, located on Ridge Avenue between 24th and 25th Streets. The Providence Grays provided the opposition in that inaugural and scored four runs in the eighth inning to beat the Phillies, 4 to 3, with future Hall of Fame pitcher "Old Hoss" Radbourn defeating John Coleman. It was the first of Radbourn's 49 victories that season, the first of Coleman's 48 defeats.

2 Q. *Which Phillies pitcher struck out the most opposing batters in one season in the National League?*

A. Steve Carlton. The lefthander struck out 310 batters in 1972, breaking the club record of 268 set by righthander Jim Bunning in 1965. Only seven major-league pitchers have fanned over 310 in one season, only two in the National League.

3 Q. *Has the Philadelphia National League club always been known as the Phillies?*

A. No. In the first year of the National League, the Philadelphia team was known as the Athletics. They were expelled from the league after that season, and the city was not represented in the National League again until 1883 when the Phillies were born, taking over the Worcester, Massachusetts, franchise. After the 1909 season, Horace Fogel, a former Philadelphia sportswriter who became president of the Phillies, decided to change the team's name to the Live Wires. The name never caught on and was soon dropped. When the Carpenter family bought the Phillies after the 1943 season, a contest was held to select a new name, and Blue Jays was picked. Although it was the official name through the 1944 season, it too was never accepted and was dropped. The 1950 Phillies, a young team that won the pennant, were also known as the Whiz Kids, although that was never an official name.

4 Q. *Starting in 1947, the Phillies have conducted spring training in Clearwater, Florida. In how many other cities have the Phillies trained?*

A. At least 21. Other Florida cities in which the Phillies have trained include St. Petersburg, Gainesville, Leesburg, Bradenton, Winter Haven, and Miami Beach. Other Phillies spring training headquarters include Charleston, South Carolina; Washington, D.C.; Richmond, Virginia; Savannah and Augusta in Georgia; Southern Pines, Wilmington, and Charlotte in North Carolina; Birmingham, Alabama; Hot Springs, Arkansas; Biloxi, Mississippi; New Braunfels, Texas; Hershey, Pennsylvania; and Wilmington, Delaware.

5 Q. *Which pitcher posted the Phillies' last victory at Philadelphia's Baker Bowl, as well as the Phillies' first victory at Shibe Park after the team moved to the home of the Philadelphia Athletics in the middle of the 1938 season?*

A. Claude Passeau. The big righthander beat the Cincinnati Reds, 10 to 3, in the first game of a doubleheader on June 26, 1938. The Phillies then lost the last four games they played at their old park, dropping the second game of the June 26 doubleheader to Cincinnati, 8 to 5, losing a doubleheader to the New York Giants, 9 to 1 and 6 to 2 June 29, and losing to the Giants, 14 to 1, June 30, with Passeau the losing pitcher. After a five-game road trip, the Phillies lost the opener of a July 4 doubleheader to the Boston Braves, 10 to 5, in the first game in their new home, but won the second game, 10 to 2, behind Passeau. The Phillies played at Shibe Park (renamed Connie Mack Stadium before the 1953 season) from July 4, 1938, through the 1970 season, then moved into Veterans Stadium.

6 Q. *Who posted the highest batting average for the Phillies in a season in which he caught at least 100 games?*

A. Spud Davis. In 1933, when he appeared in 141 games and

The Whiz Kids were a group of young Phillies who surprised the baseball world in 1950 by winning the National League pennant.

Jim Bunning fans Clarence Gaston of the Padres on May 31, 1971, in a 3 to 1 victory at San Diego for his 2,820th career strikeout, then second on the all-time list. He finished his career with 2,850.

caught 132, the righthanded-hitting Alabama native batted .349, finishing second in the National League batting race to teammate Chuck Klein, who hit .368. In his eight years with the Phillies, Davis batted over .300 six times. His .349 average is the highest ever posted by a Phillies non-outfielder.

7 Q. *In his six seasons with the Phillies, pitcher Jim Bunning started 15 games that ended with a 1 to 0 score. He won five of those games, three on home runs. Who hit those three game-winning homers?*

A. First baseman Bill White, first baseman Deron Johnson, and Bunning himself. White homered off New York Mets righthander Bob Friend on June 28, 1966, at New York's Shea Stadium, and Johnson homered off San Diego Padres righthander Al Santorini on April 25, 1970, at San Diego Stadium. On May 5, 1965, Bunning homered over the right center field fence in Shea Stadium off New York Mets lefthander Warren Spahn. It was the first National League home run of Bunning's career and the fourth of seven he would hit in his major-league career. Bunning lost eight 1 to 0 games in his six seasons with the Phillies, and was not involved in the decision in four 1 to 0 games he started.

8 Q. *Who is the only Phillies player to hit two home runs in one inning?*

A. Andy Seminick. On June 2, 1949, the righthanded-hitting catcher hit two home runs in the eighth inning as the Phillies defeated the Cincinnati Reds, 12 to 3, at Philadelphia's Shibe Park.

9 Q. *Which Phillies player was the son of a Hall of Fame first baseman?*

A. Dick Sisler. His father, George Sisler, a star first baseman from 1915 through 1930, primarily with the St. Louis Browns, was elected to the Hall of Fame in 1939. Son Dick played first base and outfield for the Phillies from 1948 through 1951 and hit the home run that won the 1950 National League pennant for the Phillies on the final day of the season in Brooklyn's Ebbets Field.

10 Q. *In 1916, Phillies pitcher Grover Cleveland Alexander set a modern major-league record for shutouts that still stands. How many shutouts did he pitch?*

A. Sixteen, a record five of them against the Cincinnati Reds. No other pitcher in this century has pitched more than 13 in one season. Alexander pitched 12 shutouts in 1915 for the second-highest total of his career, and his two-year total of 28 is seven more than any other pitcher has ever hurled in two consecutive seasons in this century.

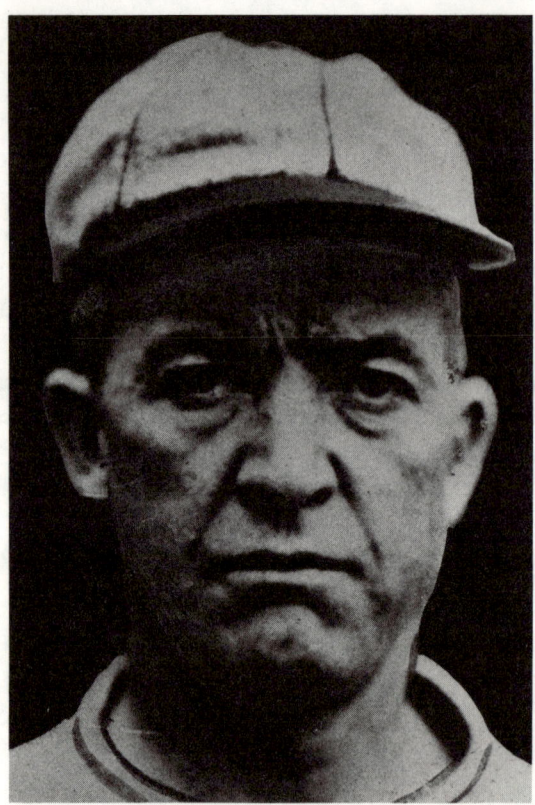

No pitcher ever won more National League games than Grover Cleveland Alexander, who starred with the Phillies from 1911 through 1917 and finished his career with 373 victories.

11 Q. *Off what pitcher did Phillies third baseman Mike Schmidt hit his first major-league home run?*

A. Balor Moore. On September 16, 1972, Schmidt hit a three-run homer off the Montreal Expos lefthander over the left field fence at Philadelphia's Veterans Stadium to give the Phillies a 3 to 1 victory. Schmidt had just been recalled from the Phillies top farm club at Eugene, Oregon, where he had 26 homers in the Pacific Coast League. That homer was Schmidt's only extra-base hit in the 13 games he played for the Phillies that season.

12 Q. *Who is the youngest player ever to play for the Phillies?*

A. Putsy Caballero. The infielder was 16 years and 10 months old when he made his major-league debut at third base for the Phillies on September 14, 1944, against the New York Giants at New York's Polo Grounds. The youngest pitcher was left-hander Rogers McKee, 16 years and 11 months old when he made his major-league debut against the St. Louis Cardinals at Philadelphia's Shibe Park on August 18, 1943. Caballero played only 322 games in his eight years with the Phillies, compiling a lifetime batting average of .228. McKee played in only five games with the Phillies in 1943 and 1944, winning his only decision.

13 Q. *How much did the value of the Phillies franchise in the National League increase in the club's first 100 years?*

A. More than $30 million. Original owners Alfred J. Reach and John I. Rogers took over the Worcester franchise after the 1882 season, held it for 20 years, and sold it for $200,000 before the 1903 season to a syndicate headed by James Potter. During the 1909 season, a syndicate headed by former sportswriter Horace Fogel bought the club for $350,000. After the 1943 season, Robert R. M. Carpenter paid $400,000 for the franchise. The Carpenter family ownership lasted for almost 38 years until the club was sold to a syndicate headed by Bill Giles for $30,175,000 in October 1981.

14 Q. *Which Phillies pitcher fulfilled his prediction that he would pick off base the first major-league player to reach base against him?*

A. Art Mahaffey. The righthander made that prediction after he was recalled from the Phillies International League farm club at Buffalo in mid-season of 1960. He made his major-league debut when he relieved in the seventh inning of a July 30 game at old Busch Stadium, St. Louis. First baseman Bill White of the St. Louis Cardinals reached first base against Mahaffey, who promptly picked him off base. Mahaffey also picked off first base the second batter who reached base against him.

Outfielder Chuck Klein joined the Phillies in 1928 and immediately became one of the National League's star sluggers. He is one of only 13 major-league players who have won the triple crown.

15 Q. *Who was the first Phillies player to get a hit in a major-league All-Star Game?*

A. Chuck Klein. In the first All-Star Game, played on July 6, 1933, at Comiskey Park, the home of the Chicago White Sox, the Phillies slugger started in right field and singled in four times at bat. The American League defeated the National League, 4 to 2.

16 Q. *Which Phillies pitcher won 99 games in his first four seasons in the National League, but never won another major-league game?*

A. Charlie Ferguson. Starting in 1884, the righthander won 21, 26, 30, and 22 games for the Phillies while losing a total of only 64. During spring training in 1888, however, the Virginian was stricken with typhoid fever and died in Philadelphia on April 29, nine days after the season started.

17 Q. *Which two former Phillies outfielders were also associated with college football's Rose Bowl?*

A. Chuck Essegian and Greasy Neale. Essegian, who played for the 1958 Phillies, also played for Stanford University in the 1952 Rose Bowl. While playing for the Los Angeles Dodgers in the 1959 World Series, he hit two home runs as a pinch-hitter to set a World Series record. Neale, who played for the Cincinnati Reds from 1916 through 1922 (except for the 22 games he played for the Phillies early in the 1921 season), was the head coach of the Washington and Jefferson 11 that tied the University of California team in the 1922 Rose Bowl. Neale later coached the Philadelphia Eagles to National Football League championships in 1948 and 1949.

18 Q. *Who was the first Phillies pitcher to wear glasses on the mound?*

A. Lee ("Specs") Meadows. The righthander, who pitched for the St. Louis Cardinals from 1915 until he was traded to the Phillies on July 14, 1919, was also the first major-league pitcher to wear glasses on the mound in this century. Meadows won 16 games for the Phillies in 1920, but enjoyed his best big-league seasons after he was traded to the Pittsburgh Pirates on May 22, 1923. The only Phillies pitcher to hurl a no-hitter while wearing glasses was Rick Wise in 1971.

19 Q. *Of the 37 men who managed the Phillies in the last 100 years, 31 played major-league baseball. How many different positions are represented?*

A. All nine. Seven were catchers, six were pitchers, nine were outfielders, split evenly among the three fields. One was a first baseman, three were second basemen, three were third basemen, and two were shortstops.

20 Q. *Name two veteran pitchers who ended their major-league careers with the Phillies and were subsequently elected to the legislatures in their home states.*

A. Jim Bunning and Larry Jackson. Bunning, who spent six of his 17 big-league seasons with the Phillies and retired as an active pitcher after the 1971 season, was later elected to the Kentucky legislature. Jackson, who spent three of his 14 big-league seasons with the Phillies and retired after the 1968 season, was later elected to the Idaho legislature. Bunning won 89 of his 224 major-league victories with the Phillies in six seasons, and Jackson won 41 of his 194 major-league victories in three seasons with the Phillies.

21 Q. *Which Phillies player struck out at the start of a triple play?*

A. Eddie Waitkus. With lefthander Al Brazle pitching for the St. Louis Cardinals on May 21, 1950, at Philadelphia's Shibe Park, I led off the last of the first inning with a single and took second on a walk to Granny Hamner. Waitkus then took a called third strike and catcher Joe Garagiola threw to third baseman Tommy Glaviano, trapping me between second and third. Shortstop Marty Marion ran me down and tagged me for the second out, then threw to first baseman Stan Musial, who tagged Hamner for the out that completed the triple play.

22 Q. *How many Phillies pitchers have been 30-game winners?*

A. Four. Charlie Ferguson won 30 games and lost nine in 1886. Kid Gleason posted a 38 and 17 win-loss record in 1890. Gus Weyhing had a 32 and 21 mark in 1892, and Grover Alexander won 30 or more games three times, with a 31 and 10 record in 1915, 33 and 12 in 1916, and 30 and 13 in 1917. All four were righthanded pitchers. The closest any Phillies pitcher has come since Alexander was in 1952, when Robin Roberts won 28 and lost seven. The closest any Phillies lefthander has come was in 1972, when Steve Carlton won 27 games and lost 10.

23 Q. *When was the "Williams Shift" first employed?*

A. In the 1920s. Although a lot of publicity was given to the "Williams Shift" used by Manager Lou Boudreau of the Cleveland Indians against Boston Red Sox slugger Ted Williams in 1946, a similar defensive alignment was first used by the Chicago Cubs against Phillies outfielder Cy Williams. The lefthanded-hitting National Leaguer was such a confirmed pull-hitter that opposing infielders shifted to the right, with the outfielders stationed in a line from the right field foul line to center field. Despite the shift, Williams hit over .300 in seven of his 13 seasons with the Phillies.

24 Q. *Who was the last Phillies pitcher to win a game in which he legally threw a spitball?*

A. Clarence Mitchell. In 1927, the lefthander won six games and lost three for the Phillies. Mitchell (who pitched for the Phillies from 1923 until he was traded to the St. Louis Cardinals on May 28, 1928) and righthander Dana Fillingim (who pitched for the Phillies in five games in 1925) were two of the 18 major-league pitchers permitted to continue throwing the spitball after the delivery was banned, along with other freak pitches, before the 1920 season. Mitchell had a 40 and 57 record with the Phillies, while Fillingim won his only decision with the Phillies in his final big-league season.

25 Q. *Who was the first Phillies player to hit a home run in an All-Star Game?*

A. John Callison. In the 37th All-Star Game, played at New York's Shea Stadium on July 7, 1964, the Phillies lefthanded-hitting outfielder entered the game as a pinch-hitter in the fifth inning and popped out, then played right field. He flied out in the seventh inning, then capped a four-run rally in the ninth inning with a two-out, three-run home run off Boston Red Sox relief ace Dick Radatz to win the game for the National League, 7 to 4. The only other All-Star Game homers by Phillies players were by Dick Allen, Greg Luzinski, and Mike Schmidt. Allen hit a solo homer in the second inning of the 1967 game at Anaheim Stadium as the National League won, 2 to 1, in 14 innings. Luzinski hit a two-run homer in the first inning of the 1977 game at New York's Yankee Stadium as the National League won, 7 to 5. Schmidt hit a game-winning, two-run homer in the eighth inning of the 1981 game at Cleveland's Municipal Stadium in the National League's 5 to 4 victory.

26 Q. *Which Phillies pitcher lost the most shutouts in one season?*

A. George McQuillan. In 1908, his first full major-league season, the righthander lost eight games in which the Phillies were shut out. Five of those shutouts were by 1 to 0 scores, tying a major-league record. McQuillan lost a total of 17 games that season and won 23, seven by shutout scores, including two by 1 to 0.

27 Q. *Who collected the most consecutive hits as a Phillies player?*

A. Ed Delahanty. In 1897, the righthanded-hitting outfielder racked up 10 hits in succession to set a National League record. Phillies Dick Sisler and Eddie Waitkus each had eight hits in a row in 1950.

28 Q. *When he was in the minor leagues, which Phillies manager spent his off-seasons as a college professor?*

A. Eddie Sawyer. Born in Westerly, Rhode Island, he attended Ithaca (New York) College, played as a minor league outfielder from 1934 through 1943, spending the last five seasons as a player-manager in the New York Yankees farm system. In the fall of 1937, he considered retiring from baseball because of a shoulder injury, got a position teaching biology and physiology at his alma mater, Ithaca, and worked toward his Master's degree. He gave up teaching at Ithaca after the 1943 season, although he coached the football team that fall at Binghamton (New York) North High School. He became a manager in the Phillies farm system in 1944 and handled their Eastern League farm club at Utica for four seasons before moving to their International League club at Toronto in 1948. Sawyer was named manager of the Phillies on July 26, 1948, and served two terms as their manager, guiding them to the National League pennant in 1950.

Eddie Sawyer, who managed the Whiz Kids to the 1950 National League pennant, throws out the ceremonial first ball before a post-season game involving the Phillies before a packed house at Veterans Stadium.

29 Q. *The Phillies are the only major-league team that has had two pitchers give up four home runs in one inning. Which pitchers, and when?*

A. In the fourth inning of the first game of a doubleheader at New York's Polo Grounds on August 13, 1939, Phillies right-handed rookie Wayne Kerksieck gave up home runs to first baseman Zeke Bonura, second baseman Alex Kampouris, pitcher Bill Lohrman, and left fielder Joe Moore; the last three were hit in succession and the New York Giants won, 11 to 2. Then on June 6, 1948, in the sixth inning of the first game of a doubleheader at Sportsman's Park, St. Louis, Phillies right-handed rookie Charlie Bicknell gave up home runs to left fielder Erv Dusak, second baseman Red Schoendienst, right fielder Enos Slaughter, and first baseman Nippy Jones as the St. Louis Cardinals won, 11 to 1.

Yielding four home runs in one inning is the major-league record. Six National League pitchers (three before the Phillies pair, and one after) share the record, along with five American League pitchers.

30 Q. *How many times did Lefty O'Doul reach base on hits, walks, and being hit by pitcher when he won the National League batting title in 1929?*

A. Three hundred, thirty-four times. The Phillies lefthanded-hitting left fielder had 254 hits, 76 walks, and was hit by pitcher four times. No National League player in this century has reached base as often.

31 Q. *In 1954, Phillies pitcher Robin Roberts gave up a home run to the first batter he faced but then retired the next 27 batters in order. Who hit the home run?*

A. Bobby Adams. The Cincinnati Reds third baseman led off the first inning of a night game on May 13, 1954, at Philadelphia's Connie Mack Stadium with a drive into the left field stands for a homer. Roberts retired every other batter who came to the plate to help the Phillies win, 8 to 1.

32 Q. *Which former Phillies player chose baseball over hockey as a professional career and spent off-seasons helping his father dig graves?*

A. Richie Hebner. A scholastic All-American hockey player at Norwood (Massachusetts) High School, as an 18-year-old Hebner was offered a contract by the Boston Bruins, but signed

In 1929, Phillies left fielder Lefty O'Doul rapped out 254 hits—a National League record. His .398 batting average that season is the highest for any Phillies player since 1900.

instead with the Pittsburgh Pirates for a $40,000 bonus in 1966. During the winter, he digs graves with his father, the foreman of a cemetery near Boston.

After eight full seasons with the Pirates, Hebner played out his option, became a free agent, and signed with the Phillies in December 1976. A third baseman with the Pirates, the left-handed-hitting Hebner was the Phillies regular first baseman in 1977 and 1978, batting over .280 each season and hitting 18 and 17 home runs. He was traded to the New York Mets before the 1979 season and has played with the Detroit Tigers and Pirates again through the 1982 season.

Richie Hebner made a successful move from third base to first base after joining the Phillies in 1977. He moved on in 1979.

33 Q. *What pitcher hurled the most innings in one game for the Phillies?*

A. Mule Watson. At Chicago's Cubs Park on July 17, 1918, the righthander gave up a run in the first inning and a run in the 21st inning as the Phillies lost to the Chicago Cubs, 2 to 1. Watson gave up 18 singles and a double, while winning pitcher George Tyler, who also pitched a complete game, yielded 12 singles, a double, and a run in the fourth inning.

Two other Phillies pitchers have worked a 20-inning game. Tully Sparks pitched all the way in a 2 to 1 loss in 20 innings to Chicago at home on August 24, 1905, and Joe Oeschger pitched all 20 innings in a 9 to 9 tie with the Brooklyn Dodgers at home on April 30, 1919.

34 Q. *What is the Phillies highest season total of one-run victories in this century?*

A. Thirty-seven. In 1968, the Phillies won 76 games, 37 of them by one run. Of their 86 defeats that season, 29 were by one run. The pennant-winning 1950 Phillies had a 29 and 16 record, and the 1980 world champion Phillies had a 32 and 28 log in one-run games.

35 Q. *All-time, major-league home run king Hank Aaron hit the 400th and 700th home runs of his career off lefthanded Phillies pitchers. Name them.*

A. Bo Belinsky and Ken Brett. Belinsky served up the 400th on April 20, 1966, at Philadelphia's Connie Mack Stadium as the Atlanta Braves beat the Phillies, 8 to 1. Brett gave up the 700th on July 21, 1973, at Atlanta-Fulton County Stadium in an 8 to 3 Phillies victory. The first Phillies pitcher to give up a home run to Aaron was Robin Roberts—on June 26, 1954, at Connie Mack Stadium, during a 10 to 3 Phillies victory over the Milwaukee Braves.

36 Q. *In the first three seasons he pitched against the New York Mets at Shea Stadium, what was the remarkable record Phillies pitcher Jim Bunning put together?*

A. Eight starts and eight complete-game victories. The first game the righthander ever pitched at Shea Stadium was a perfect game, the first game of a doubleheader won by the Phillies, 6 to 0, June 21, 1964. His next start at Shea resulted in a 6 to 1 victory on August 14 in the first game of a twilight-night doubleheader. In 1965, Bunning won at Shea by scores of 1 to 0, 5 to 1, and 6 to 0; in 1966 he won at Shea by scores of 7 to 2, 1 to 0, and 6 to 0, with one unearned run in the 7 to 2 victory. The streak ended April 21, 1967, when the Mets chased Bunning in the second inning of a 6 to 3 triumph. But in his final start at Shea that season, he came back to pitch a 1 to 0 victory.

37 Q. *In what season in which the Phillies played over 150 games did the leading winner on the pitching staff win only eight games?*

A. In 1928. Righthander Ray Benge had an 8 and 18 record to lead the club in victories. The Phillies employed 16 pitchers that season; five of them failed to win a game, while eight others won fewer than six games. Top winners behind Benge on the last-place club were righthanders Bob McGraw (7 and 8) and Claude Willoughby (6 and 5), the latter being the only pitcher on the staff with a winning record.

38 Q. *Which Phillies rookie marred the major-league debut of one of the 1960s' most successful National League pitchers?*

A. Clay Dalrymple. On July 19, 1960, the rookie catcher batted for Phillies catcher Cal Neeman with the bases empty and two out in the eighth inning. He lined a single to center for the only Phillies hit off Juan Marichal during the rookie righthander's first game for the San Francisco Giants at San Francisco's Candlestick Park. In his 2 to 0 victory, Marichal struck out 12 and walked only one. He went on to win 243 games in his major-league career and in six seasons won 20 or more games.

39 Q. *Which Phillies pitcher in this century won the most games in a season in which he failed to pitch a shutout?*

A. Jimmy Ring. The righthander, who pitched for the Phillies from 1921 through 1925 and again in 1928, won 18 games in 1923 without pitching a shutout. He lost 16 games, pitched 23 complete games, and had an earned-run average of 3.76. This was the third year in a row Ring failed to pitch a shutout. In his six seasons with the Phillies, he won 68 games but pitched only two shutouts.

40 Q. *What is the highest number of hits collected in one month by a Phillies player in this century?*

A. Sixty-one. In July 1930, right fielder Chuck Klein tallied 32 singles, 18 doubles, one triple, and 10 home runs, batting .455 in 33 games for the month.

41 Q. *During his major-league career off which pitcher did Pete Rose hit his only bases-loaded home run?*

A. Dallas Green. On July 18, 1964, Rose, then the Cincinnati Reds second baseman, hit a grand-slam homer into the right field stands at Crosley Field in the fifth inning of a game the Phillies lost to the Reds, 14 to 4. Fifteen years later, Rose became the Phillies first baseman, playing a key role in the Phillies' 1980 world championship under Dallas Green's managership.

Dallas Green managed the Phillies to their first World Series championship in 1980. Before taking over the managing job late in 1979, Green pitched for the Phillies and ran their farm system.

42 Q. *Which other players hit grand-slam home runs off Dallas Green during his Phillies career?*

A. Ron Santo and Jim Pagliaroni. On August 14, 1960, Chicago Cubs third baseman Santo homered with the bases loaded in the sixth inning of the second game of a doubleheader at Philadelphia's Connie Mack Stadium. The Cubs won, 7 to 3. At Pittsburgh's Forbes Field on May 26, 1964, in a game

Reserve outfielder-first baseman Del Unser collected clutch hits to help the Phillies win the 1980 pennant and World Series.

won by the Pittsburgh Pirates, 13 to 4, catcher Pagliaroni hit a bases-loaded homer in the second inning.

43 Q. *What pinch-hitting record did Del Unser set in 1979 with the Phillies?*

A. He pinch-hit three home runs in a row. The lefthanded-hitting outfielder-first baseman hit a home run on June 30 at Busch Stadium, St. Louis, to help the Phillies defeat the St. Louis Cardinals, 6 to 4. On July 5 at Philadelphia's Veterans Stadium, he hit a home run as the Phillies lost to the New York Mets, 3 to 2. And on July 10 at Veterans Stadium, he hit a home run in the Phillies' 6 to 5 victory over the San Diego Padres. For the season, Unser had four home runs, 14 hits, 14 runs batted in and a .304 batting average as a pinch-hitter.

44 Q. *Who are the only National League players who have been unanimous choices for the Most Valuable Player Award?*

A. Orlando Cepeda and Mike Schmidt. Cepeda, first baseman of the world-champion St. Louis Cardinals, received every first-place vote in 1967; Schmidt, third baseman of the world-champion Phillies, made a clean sweep in 1980.

45 Q. *Since 1900, who holds the Phillies record for stolen bases?*

A. Sherry Magee. The Phillies left fielder stole 55 bases in 1906 to finish only two behind National League leader Frank Chance of the Chicago Cubs. Magee also stole 48 in 1905, 46 in 1907, and 49 in 1910, yet never led the league. Third baseman Hans Lobert stole 41 bases in 1913, but no Phillies player since then has reached the 40-mark in steals until rookie Bob Dernier stole 42 in 1982.

46 Q. *How many Phillies pitchers have hit two home runs in one game?*

A. Five. First, Jack Knight hit two homers in the first game of a doubleheader at New York's Polo Grounds on June 24, 1926,

Lefthander Randy Lerch was a regular starter for the Phillies at age 22, but never realized his full potential. His biggest victory was the 1978 division-clinching game when he hit two home runs.

in a 12 to 7 loss to the Giants. Second, Phil Collins hit a pair at Philadelphia's Baker Bowl on July 22, 1930, in an 11 to 5 victory over the Pittsburgh Pirates. Third, Rick Wise hit two at Cincinnati's Riverfront Stadium on June 23, 1971, in a 4 to 0 no-hit victory over the Cincinnati Reds. Wise also hit two at Philadelphia's Veterans Stadium on August 28, 1971, in a 7 to 3 victory over the San Francisco Giants in the second game of a twilight-night doubleheader. Fourth, Larry Christenson hit two at New York's Shea Stadium on September 5, 1976, in a 3 to 1 victory over the Mets. And fifth, Randy Lerch hit two at Pittsburgh's Three River Stadium on September 30, 1978, in a 10 to 8 victory over the Pittsburgh Pirates. All but Knight and Lerch were righthanded hitters.

47 Q. *When the Phillies won the National League pennant in 1980, how many days of the regular season did they spend in first place?*

A. Eighteen, although they were tied for two of those days. On September 1 at San Francisco's Candlestick Park, the Phillies took over first place by defeating the San Francisco Giants, 6 to 4, and remained in first place for nine days in September. By beating the Montreal Expos, 2 to 1, at Montreal's Olympic Stadium October 3, the Phillies took over first place for the last time and clinched the Eastern Divison title the next night with a 6 to 4 victory over the Expos in 11 innings.

48 Q. *What was unusual about the first inning of the opening game of the 1938 season between the Phillies and the Brooklyn Dodgers?*

A. A rookie on each team hit a home run on his first time at bat in the major leagues. In the top of that first inning at Philadelphia's Baker Bowl on April 19, 1938, Brooklyn center fielder Ernie Koy hit a home run. In the bottom of the same inning, Phillies second baseman Emmett Mueller homered. The Dodgers won the game, 12 to 5.

49 Q. *Who holds the major-league record for making 400 or more outfield putouts in a season for the most years?*

A. I do. While I played center field with the Phillies, I had more than 400 putouts in every season from 1949 through 1958, except for 1955. I also hold the major-league record for most years with 500 or more putouts (4), and I'm tied with Max Carey for most years leading the league in chances accepted (9) and putouts (9).

50 Q. *Since Grover Alexander was traded to the Chicago Cubs after the 1917 season, who is the only Phillies pitcher to hurl more than 30 complete games in a season?*

A. Robin Roberts. The righthander pitched 33 complete games in 1953 when he won 23 games and lost 16. He led the National League in complete games in 1952 with 30, in 1953, in 1954 with 29, in 1955 with 26, and in 1956 with 22. Alexander also led the league in complete games five times while with the Phillies, starting in 1911, his rookie season. His complete game totals with which he led the league were 31 in 1911, 32 in 1914, 36 in 1915, 38 in 1916, and 35 in 1917. The only other Phillies pitcher to lead the league in complete games is Steve Carlton, who led with 30 in 1972, tied for the lead with 18 in 1973, and led with 19 in 1982.

The premier National League pitcher of the 1950s was Phillies ace Robin Roberts, a 20-game winner six seasons in a row.

51 Q. *Who was the first Phillies player to win a National League batting championship?*

A. Billy Hamilton. In 1891, the left fielder batted .340 to win the title by 21 points over Cincinnati Reds center fielder Bug Holliday. Hamilton also won in 1893 with a .380 average. I was the only other Phillies player to win the batting title twice.

52 Q. *On the morning of September 21, 1964, when the Phillies had a six and one-half game lead with 12 games left to play, but failed to win the National League pennant, what was their "magic number"?*

A. Seven. Any combination of Phillies victories and defeats for each of the two teams tied for second place totaling seven would have given the Phillies the pennant. The St. Louis Cardinals and Cincinnati Reds were tied for second place with identical 83 and 66 records when the final two weeks of the season began, and the fourth-place San Francisco Giants were another half-game back with an 83 and 67 record. However, the Phillies lost 10 games in a row before winning the final two games of the season. St. Louis won the pennant with a 93 and 69 record. The Phillies and Cincinnati finished with 92 and 70 records and San Francisco was fourth with a 90 and 72 record.

53 Q. *Which Phillies relief pitcher once struck out six batters in succession in one game?*

A. Jack Meyer. On September 22, 1958, in the first game of a twilight-night doubleheader against the Pittsburgh Pirates at Philadelphia's Connie Mack Stadium, the hard-throwing right-hander relieved Dick Farrell at the start of the 12th inning with the score tied at 2 to 2, and struck out the first six batters he faced. In all, Phillies starter Seth Morehead, Farrell, and Meyer struck out 21 Pirates to set the major-league record at that time for strikeouts by one team in an extra-inning game. The Phillies eventually scored in the 14th inning to win, 3 to 2.

54 Q. *Who was the first outfielder in major-league history to play in more than 150 games in a season and finish with a 1.000 fielding percentage for the season?*

A. Danny Litwhiler. In 1942, the Phillies left fielder played 151 games in the outfield, making 308 putouts and nine assists without an error. Only two other National League outfielders have matched Litwhiler's perfect record for 150 or more games. During that 1942 season, Litwhiler also led the Phillies in doubles, triples, home runs, and runs batted in; he also paced the club's regulars in batting average and slugging percentage.

55 Q. *In what season did the Phillies win the most night games?*

A. In 1977. That season, the Phillies won the National League's Eastern Divison title by winning 101 games: they won 71 night games, and lost only 39. The 1950 pennant-winning Phillies had a 36 and 19 record in night games, and the 1980 world champion Phillies had a 66 and 46 record at night.

56 Q. *Who was the most recent Phillies player to hit a home run in every National League park in a season?*

A. Mike Schmidt. In 1979, when the righthanded-hitting third baseman hit 45 home runs to finish second in the league, he hit at least one homer in each of the 12 National League parks. Before Schmidt, the last Phillies player to hit a home run in every National League park was outfielder Wally Post. In 1959, he hit only 22 homers, but hit 11 in Philadelphia's Connie Mack Stadium, three in the Los Angeles Coliseum, two each in Milwaukee County Stadium and in Chicago's Wrigley Field, and one each in Cincinnati's Crosley Field, Pittsburgh's Forbes Field, San Francisco's Seals Stadium, and St. Louis's old Busch Stadium.

57 Q. *In addition to being the all-time Phillies leader in victories, Robin Roberts is first in how many of the club's other major pitching categories?*

A. Six. The righthander, who won 234 games in his 14 seasons with the Phillies, also pitched the most games (529), lost the most games (199), completed the most games (272), pitched the most innings (3,740), gave up the most hits (3,661), and yielded the most runs (1,591).

58 Q. *In this century, how many Phillies players have led the National League in stolen bases?*

A. Three. Right fielder Chuck Klein led with 20 stolen bases in 1932, second baseman Danny Murtaugh led with 18 in 1941, and I led with 32 in 1948, my rookie season.

59 Q. *How many times has Steve Carlton pitched in relief in his 11 seasons with the Phillies?*

A. None. The lefthander has relieved only 18 times in his major-league career, which began in 1965 with the St. Louis Cardinals, but has been used only as a starting pitcher since he was traded to the Phillies before the 1972 season.

60 Q. *In how many seasons did the Phillies use more than one manager?*

A. Sixteen. The first manager replaced during the season was Bob Ferguson, succeeded after only 17 games by Blondie Purcell in 1883. In 1898, Bill Shettsline replaced George Stallings. In 1919, Gavvy Cravath took over for Jack Coombs. In 1921, Bill Donovan started the season and Kaiser Wilhelm finished it. After that, Jimmie Wilson was replaced by Hans Lobert in 1938, Bucky Harris by Fred Fitzsimmons in 1943, Fitzsimmons by Ben Chapman in 1945, Chapman by Eddie Sawyer in 1948, Sawyer by Steve O'Neill in 1952, O'Neill by Terry Moore in 1954, Mayo Smith by Sawyer in 1958, Sawyer by Gene Mauch in 1960, Mauch by Bob Skinner in 1968, Skinner by George Myatt in 1969, Frank Lucchesi by Paul Owens in 1972, and Danny Ozark by Dallas Green in 1979.

Having a disagreement with Umpire Ed Vargo is Danny Ozark, who managed the Phillies to division titles in 1976, 1977, and 1978.

61 Q. *Which Phillies pitcher holds the modern National League record for pitching the most one-hit games in one season?*

A. Grover Alexander. The righthander pitched four one-hit games in 1915: June 5 at St. Louis, June 26 against Brooklyn, July 5 against New York, and September 29 at Boston. Alexander finished his career with 373 victories, tied with Christy Mathewson for the most in National League history, but never pitched a no-hit game.

62 Q. *What former University of Michigan football captain later played for the Phillies?*

A. John Herrnstein. The lefthanded outfielder–first baseman, who signed with the Phillies for a $40,000 bonus, made his major-league debut with the Phillies in 1962, and was the first baseman used in the most games for the Phillies in 1964. He was traded to the Chicago Cubs in April 1966.

63 Q. *Which pitcher started his major-league career with the Phillies before the turn of the century and had the unusual nickname of "The Curveless Wonder"?*

A. Al Orth. The righthander from Indiana, who won 98 games and lost 67 for the Phillies from 1895 through 1901, was given that nickname because he threw almost all fast balls. He won his first eight major-league decisions in 1895, won 20 games in 1901, then jumped to the new Washington Senators of the American League. For a pitcher, Orth hit well and played as an outfielder for the Phillies in 15 games in seven years. Three times with the Phillies, the lefthanded batter hit over .300; his overall average for his years with the Phillies was .294.

64 Q. *Who holds the Phillies club record for hitting in the most consecutive games in this century?*

A. Chuck Klein. In 1930, the lefthanded-hitting right fielder set the club record by hitting in 26 straight games from May 18 through June 17, then tied his own record later that season by hitting safely in 26 more games from July 12 through August 3. In that same season, Klein had three 14-game hitting streaks and batted safely in 135 of the Phillies' 156 games. Before 1900, outfielder Billy Hamilton hit safely in 36 straight games in 1894, and outfielder Ed Delahanty hit safely in 31 games in a row in 1899.

The longest streak since Klein's two in 1930 was by center fielder Willie Montanez, who hit safely in 24 straight games from July 9 through the first game of a doubleheader on August 4, 1974.

65 Q. *Who was the last non-pitcher to play for the Phillies who also played for the Philadelphia Athletics?*

A. Elmer Valo. The lefthanded-hitting outfielder started his major-league career with the A's and played for them in Philadelphia from 1940 through 1954. After playing for the Phillies for part of the 1956 season and part of the 1961 season, he retired. In recent years, he has been a scout for the Phillies.

66 Q. *In the four no-hit games by Phillies pitchers and the 17 pitched against the Phillies in this century, how many home runs have pitchers hit?*

A. Only two, both by Phillies pitcher Rick Wise in his no-hitter at Cincinnati's Riverfront Stadium on June 23, 1971. In his 4 to 0 victory over the Cincinnati Reds, the righthanded hitter lined a Ross Grimsley pitch over the left field fence with Roger Freed on base in the fifth inning, then hit a Clay Carroll pitch over the same fence with no one on base in the eighth inning. The only batter to reach base against Wise was shortstop Dave Concepción, who walked on a 3 and 1 pitch with one out in the sixth inning.

The only other pitchers to hit a home run in a no-hitter are Wes Ferrell of the Cleveland Indians in 1931, Jim Tobin of the Boston Braves in 1944, and Earl Wilson of the Boston Red Sox in 1962. Wise's two-homer feat in a no-hit game has never been done before or since.

67 Q. *Who hit 19 home runs in his career with the Phillies, four with the bases loaded?*

A. Vince DiMaggio. The righthanded-hitting center fielder hit four grand-slam homers in 1945 to tie what was then the major-league record. He played in 127 games for the Phillies that season, and in six in 1946 before he was traded to the New York Giants May 1, 1946. The club record for grand-slam home runs in a career is six, set by outfielder Cy Williams and matched by outfielder Chuck Klein and third baseman Willie Jones.

68 Q. *For what feat is Phillies pitcher Bill Duggleby remembered?*

A. A grand-slam home run in his first major-league at-bat. On April 21, 1898, the righthander hit the homer in the second inning against the New York Giants. Until then, no National League player had ever hit a home run in his first time at bat—and it was more than 70 years before any player hit a grand-slam homer in his first major-league game. On June 25, 1968, outfielder Bobby Bonds of the San Francisco Giants hit a bases-loaded homer on his third time at bat in the sixth inning of a 9 to 0 victory over the Los Angeles Dodgers in San Francisco's Candlestick Park.

69 Q. *Which Phillies pitcher won a season opener, 1 to 0, and scored the winning run?*

A. Les Sweetland. The lefthander doubled in the eighth inning and scored on Chuck Klein's single off Brooklyn Dodgers righthander Watty Clark at Brooklyn's Ebbets Field on April 15, 1930. Sweetland allowed only three hits, retiring the last 21 batters in order for his only shutout of the season, his third and last shutout of his five-year, major-league career. The 1 to 0 score in the opening game gave no hint that the 1930 season would be a tremendous year for hitting: as a whole, the National League batted .303 that season.

70 Q. *Which Phillies catcher stole the most bases in one season?*

A. Red Dooin. The speedy righthanded hitter stole 20 bases in 1908. Dooin, who caught for the Phillies from 1902 through 1914, and was a player-manager the last five of those seasons, also holds the career record for stolen bases by a catcher while with the Phillies, having swiped 132 in 1,218 games.

71 Q. *Who was the only pitcher to win 20 games for both the Phillies and Philadelphia Athletics?*

A. Chick Fraser. The righthander had a 21 and 13 record in 1899, his first season with the Phillies, and a 20 and 15 record in 1901, his only season with the Athletics. He returned to the Phillies in 1902, but never won more than 15 games in any other season.

72 Q. *In their 10-game losing streak in the final two weeks of the 1964 season—a slump that cost the Phillies the National League pennant—how many runs did the Phillies score?*

A. Thirty-four. They were shut out, 1 to 0, in the first game of the losing streak, by the Cincinnati Reds at Philadelphia's Connie Mack Stadium, but scored two or more runs in eight of the other nine games, with a high of eight runs in a 14 to 8 loss to the Milwaukee Braves on September 27 at Connie Mack

Stadium. That defeat knocked the Phillies out of first place for the first time since July 15.

73 Q. *Which Phillies pitcher was named after a United States president?*

A. Grover Cleveland Alexander. Born on February 26, 1887, on a farm in St. Paul, Nebraska, he was named for our 22nd president.

74 Q. *Who managed the Phillies for the most seasons?*

A. Harry Wright. He managed the Phillies for 10 full seasons from 1884 through 1893. Second was Gene Mauch, manager for almost eight and one-half seasons, starting in 1960 and

Fiery Gene Mauch managed the Phillies in more games than anyone and barely missed winning the 1964 pennant. He took over as manager after two games in 1960 and remained until June, 1968.

ending midway through the 1968 season. Close behind Mauch was Danny Ozark, who managed the Phillies from 1972 until he was replaced by Dallas Green on August 31, 1979. In winning percentage, Ozark heads this trio with a .538 mark, having won 594 games; Wright is second with a .534 percentage and 678 victories, and Mauch is third with a .485 percentage and 645 victories.

75 Q. *The Phillies are one of only three teams in National League history to hit five home runs in one inning. Which pitcher hit one of the Phillies five home runs in the eighth inning of a 1949 game?*

A. Schoolboy Rowe. The righthander, who won the game from the Cincinnati Reds, 12 to 3, on June 2, 1949, at Philadelphia's Connie Mack Stadium, hit a home run after Del Ennis, Andy Seminick, and Willie Jones homered. After Rowe homered, Seminick hit his second home run of the inning. Homers by Ennis and Seminick at the start of the inning came off Cincinnati lefthander Ken Raffensberger. His successor, righthander Jess Dobernic, gave up home runs to Jones and Rowe, and lefthander Kent Peterson yielded the second homer of the inning to Seminick. Peterson was also tagged for a double by Granny Hamner that hit a foot or two from the top of the left field wall, and a triple by Jones that missed being a home run by inches. The Phillies had 26 total bases in the inning, and scored 10 runs.

76 Q. *Nine times, the Phillies have shut out an opponent in both games of a doubleheader. Who were the winning pitchers in the most recent shutout sweep?*

A. Frank Sullivan and Art Mahaffey. On April 23, 1961, Sullivan shut out the Chicago Cubs, 1 to 0, in the first game, and Mahaffey blanked the Cubs, 6 to 0, in the second game at Philadelphia's Connie Mack Stadium. On October 2, 1965, at New York's Shea Stadium, the Phillies shut out the New York Mets, 6 to 0, in the first game of a twilight-night doubleheader, but the second game ended in a 0 to 0 tie after being halted by the New York State curfew law after 18 innings.

77 Q. *Who played shortstop for the Phillies and later pitched for the Athletics?*

A. Granny Hamner. Signed by the Phillies in 1944 as a 17-year-old, Hamner became the Phillies regular shortstop in 1948 and stayed with the club until he was traded to the Cleveland Indians in 1959. Late in his career, the righthander developed a knuckleball and pitched in four games for the Phillies. He later returned to the minor leagues to develop his pitching skills, and joined the Kansas City Athletics as a pitcher in 1962, relieving in three games before retiring.

Granny Hamner made his debut with the Phillies as a 17-year-old in 1944. He was their star shortstop before and after the Whiz Kids won the 1950 pennant, and ended his career as a pitcher.

78 Q. *How many Phillies pitchers have lost 20 or more games in the season after each won 20 games?*

A. Two. Eppa Rixey had a 22 and 10 record for the Phillies in 1916, and a 16 and 21 record in 1917; Steve Carlton had a 27 and 10 record in 1972, and a 13 and 20 record in 1973. Both lefthanders bounced back to become 20-game winners later in their careers.

79 Q. *Who was the first major-league catcher to wear shinguards?*

A. Red Dooin. Roger Bresnahan of the New York Giants is generally credited with having invented shinguards and wearing them in a game for the first time in 1908. But Dooin, who caught for the Phillies from 1902 through 1914, wore them under his stockings as early as 1906. "Bresnahan always got the credit," Dooin said, "but I used them a couple of years before he even dreamed of them. I had a special type made, substituting pâpier maché for rattan to make them lighter."

80 Q. *Which Phillies pitcher hurled a complete game and pitched the most innings in a scoreless game?*

A. Joe Oeschger. On September 4, 1917, at Brooklyn's Ebbets Field, the Phillies righthander and Brooklyn Dodgers righthander Jeff Pfeffer both pitched 14 scoreless innings before the game was called. On October 2, 1965, at New York's Shea Stadium, lefthander Chris Short pitched 15 scoreless innings in the second game of a twilight-night doubleheader against the New York Mets in a game that ended 0 to 0 after 18 innings. In 1907, righthander Lew Richie pitched a complete game against the Chicago Cubs that ended in a 10-inning scoreless tie. In 1913, Grover Alexander pitched all 11 innings against the New York Giants, and all 10 innings against the Boston Braves in games that ended in scoreless ties. And in 1953, Bob Miller pitched all 10 innings against the Milwaukee Braves in another 0 to 0 deadlock.

81 Q. *Which major-league team has scored in the most no-hit games pitched against them in this century?*

A. The Phillies. Three times, the Phillies were held hitless for nine innings but managed to score a run. In 1925, Dazzy Vance of the Brooklyn Dodgers no-hit the Phillies and won, 10 to 1. In 1963, Don Nottebart of the Houston Colt 45s no-hit them in a 4 to 1 victory; and in 1968, George Culver of the Cincinnati Reds held them hitless and won, 6 to 1. In each of these games, the Phil who scored reached base on an error and eventually scored on a sacrifice fly.

Jack Clements was a rarity in the major leagues. The Philadelphian was the best of the lefthanded-throwing catchers before 1900, and spent nine of his 17 big-league seasons as the Phillies regular.

82 Q. *Who was the first major-league catcher to wear a chest protector?*

A. Jack Clements. The lefthanded-throwing receiver, a Philadelphian, first wore a protector with the Philadelphia Keystones of the Union Association in 1884. He joined the Phillies late that season, staying with them through 1897.

83 Q. *What is the highest number of singles collected in one season by a Phillies player?*

A. One hundred, eighty-one. Left fielder Lefty O'Doul had 181 singles in 254 hits in 1929, and I hit 181 singles in 221 hits in 1951. A center fielder, I also led the National League in singles while with the Phillies in 1953 with 169, in 1957 with 152, and in 1958 with 176, as well as in 1951. In 1929, O'Doul and Pittsburgh's Lloyd Waner led with 181. Waner set the modern major-league record with 198 singles in 1927.

84 Q. *Who hit the Phillies' first World Series home run?*

A. Fred Luderus. The first baseman hit a pitch by Rube Foster of the Boston Red Sox over the right field wall at Philadelphia's Baker Bowl with one out and nobody on base in the fourth inning of the fifth game of the 1915 World Series. The homer gave the Phillies a 3 to 2 lead, but the Red Sox came back to win the game, 5 to 4, and the World Series.

Sixty-five years later, the second Phillies World Series home run was hit by Bake McBride. The right fielder hit a three-run homer in the third inning of the first game of the 1980 World Series against the Kansas City Royals, putting the Phillies ahead to stay in a 7 to 6 victory. The only other Phillies home runs in World Series play were by third baseman Mike Schmidt in the third and fifth games in 1980.

85 Q. *How many triple plays did the Phillies execute in 1964?*

A. Three, equalling the major-league record. On May 17 at Houston's Colts Stadium, the Phillies made their first triple play in almost six years as Jerry Grote of the Houston Colt 45s grounded to first baseman John Herrnstein with runners on first and second. Herrnstein threw to second for the first out, then took shortstop Bobby Wine's return throw for the second out. Herrnstein threw to catcher Clay Dalrymple, who tagged Rusty Staub, trying to score from second on the play, to end the inning.

On August 15 at New York's Shea Stadium, Bobby Klaus of the New York Mets lined to pitcher John Boozer for the first out with runners on first and second. Boozer threw to shortstop Ruben Amaro, and the relay to first baseman Frank Thomas tripled the runner off first to complete the second-inning triple play.

On October 2 at Cincinnati's Crosley Field, Deron Johnson of the Cincinnati Reds lined out to left fielder Alex Johnson with runners on first and second in the fourth inning. Vada Pinson was doubled off second, Johnson to shortstop Bobby Wine to second baseman Tony Taylor, and Frank Robinson was tripled off first when Taylor relayed the ball to first baseman Vic Power. The Phillies won the games by scores of 2 to 0, 8 to 1, and 4 to 3, respectively.

Deron Johnson played for nine major-league clubs in 16 seasons, more than four of them with the Phillies, for whom he was a home run and runs-batted-in leader. He's now a Phillies coach.

86 Q. *In what year did the Phillies have two 20-game winning pitchers and yet finished in the National League's second division?*

A. In 1914. Grover Alexander won 27 games and Erskine Mayer won 21 that season, but the Phillies won only 74 games and finished sixth. They won their first National League pennant the next season.

87 Q. *Four Phillies outfielders have played 100 or more games in a season without an error. Who were they?*

A. Danny Litwhiler, Tony Gonzalez, Don Demeter, and John Callison. Litwhiler played 151 errorless games in the outfield in 1942. Gonzalez was in 114 games in 1962, Demeter in 119 in 1963, and Callison in 109 in 1968. Only three other outfielders in the modern history of the National League have played in more than 100 games without an error, and no players have ever done it at any other position.

88 Q. *When pitcher Steve Carlton won 15 straight games for the Phillies in 1972, how many complete games did he pitch in the streak?*

A. Fourteen. The streak's only incomplete game was the first. On June 7 in a 3 to 1 Phillies victory over the Houston Astros at Philadelphia's Veterans Stadium, Carlton was removed for a pinch-hitter in the seventh inning because of a slight muscle pull in his back. Four days later, Carlton went the route to beat the Atlanta Braves, 3 to 1, and his next 13 victories were all complete games. The winning streak ended August 21 at Veterans Stadium in an 11-inning, 2 to 1 defeat in which winning pitcher Phil Niekro of the Atlanta Braves and Carlton both pitched complete games. During his winning streak, Carlton made no-decision starts on June 16, June 21, and July 15.

89 Q. *When the Phillies took over the Worcester franchise after the 1882 season, which was the most difficult team for them to defeat?*

A. Boston. The Phillies lost all 14 games they played with Boston in 1883, and the first seven meetings in 1884 before they finally won, 7 to 2, on June 17 as Charlie Ferguson beat Jim Whitney. In the 21 straight games the Phillies lost to Boston, Whitney and Charlie Buffinton each won 10 of the games and John Morrill won the other. Morrill was primarily a first baseman and the game he won from the Phillies was his only big-league career victory. In 1883 and 1884, Boston had a combined 27 and 3 record against the Phillies, including a 14 and 1 mark in Philadelphia.

90 Q. *Which Phillies pitcher holds the major-league record for the most consecutive scoreless innings at the start of a career?*

A. George McQuillan. The righthander made his major-league debut on May 8, 1907, went to the minors, and returned late in the season to pitch on September 22, 25, and 29, putting together a string of 25 scoreless innings for a record that still stands. He relieved once, started four games, and posted a 4 and 0 record that season. He was a 23-game winner in 1908, his first full big-league season.

91 Q. *Which former Phillies pitcher set a World Series record by appearing in all seven games with another team?*

A. Darold Knowles, who relieved in 69 games for the Phillies in 1966, relieved in all seven games of the 1973 World Series to help the Oakland Athletics beat the New York Mets.

92 Q. *How many Phillies have hit more than 30 home runs in four consecutive seasons?*

A. Two. Right fielder Chuck Klein hit 43 in 1929, 40 in 1930, 31 in 1931, and 38 in 1932. Third baseman Mike Schmidt hit 36 in 1974, 38 in 1975, 38 in 1976, and 38 in 1977, then did it again starting with 45 in 1979, and a career high 48 in 1980, then hit 31 in 1981 and 35 in 1982.

93 Q. *In 1957, future Hall of Famer Robin Roberts tied what was then the Phillies club record for strikeouts in a nine-inning game. How many did he strike out?*

A. Thirteen. On May 2, 1957, at Philadelphia's Connie Mack Stadium, Roberts struck out 13 Chicago Cubs in a 4 to 2 victory. The club record was broken four seasons later. In his first pro season, on June 5, 1948, while pitching for the Phillies' Wilmington farm club, Roberts tied the Inter-State League record by striking out 18 Trenton batters in a 4 to 1 victory.

94 Q. Which promising young Phillies catcher was killed while walking along a sidewalk in Baltimore more than half a century ago?

A. Walter Lerian. The 26-year-old Baltimore native had been the Phillies first-string catcher in 1928 and 1929. He was killed when a truck hit him in his home city on October 22, 1929.

95 Q. What was the Phillies' most successful month in the past 60 years?

A. May 1976. That month, the Phillies won 22 games and lost only five for a winning percentage of .815. The Phillies also won 22 games in September 1916, July 1950, and July 1952, but lost nine, 13, and 10, respectively, in those years. In each of those months the winning percentage was more than .100 points below the club record.

96 Q. What was the most unsuccessful month for the Phillies in the past 60 years?

A. May 1928. The Phillies won only three games and lost 22 that month to set a National League record for the lowest monthly winning percentage—.120. In September 1939, the Phillies lost 27 games and won only six for a .182 percentage. The 27 losses tied a National League record for a month.

97 Q. In 1980, when the Phillies began the surge that eventually led to the division title, as well as the club's third pennant and first world championship, how many games were they behind the National League's Eastern Division leader?

A. Six. After losing a four-game weekend series to the Pittsburgh Pirates at Pittsburgh's Three Rivers Stadium August 8 through 10, the Phillies not only trailed by six games, but were also only three games over .500 with a 55 and 52 record. They won 36 of their next 54 games to win the division championship, their fourth in five years. For the first time, the Phillies won the Championship Series, defeating the Western Division champion Houston Astros three games to two to win the pennant. They went on to beat the American League champion Kansas City Royals in the World Series, four games to two.

98 Q. *Which Phillies pitcher came closest to pitching a no-hit, no-run game in the opening game of a season?*

A. Robin Roberts. On April 13, 1955, opening day, at Philadelphia's Connie Mack Stadium, the future Hall of Fame

Down but not out is Phillies second baseman Dave Cash in a game with the Chicago Cubs. Obtained in a trade with Pittsburgh in 1973, Cash averaged better than 200 hits in his three years with the Phils.

righthander had a no-hitter and a 4 to 0 lead over the New York Giants with one out in the ninth inning. Shortstop Al Dark then slapped an 0 and 2 pitch into right field for a clean single and the first hit. In the same inning, Monte Irvin hit a two-run double and Hank Thompson beat out an infield hit before Roberts got the third out to win the game, 4 to 2.

99 Q. Since 1900, seven Phillies have led the National League in hits a total of 10 times. Five of the seven were outfielders. What positions did the other two play?

A. Second base and first base. In 1975, second baseman Dave Cash led the league with 213 hits; in the strike-shortened 1981 season, first baseman Pete Rose led with 140.

100 Q. In the fourth inning of the opening game of the 1915 World Series, what was unusual about the hit that Phillies left fielder Possum Whitted beat out to Boston Red Sox second baseman Jack Barry?

A. It batted in the first run the Phillies ever scored in a World Series game. It was Whitted's only hit in his 17 plate appearances in the five games of that World Series.

101 Q. Who was the last major-league pitcher to pitch two complete games in one day?

A. Jack Scott. The Phillies righthander, then 35 and the oldest ever to pitch two complete games in one day, beat the Cincinnati Reds, 3 to 1, in the first game of the doubleheader, then lost the second game, 3 to 0, to lefthander Eppa Rixey on June 19, 1927, at Cincinnati's Redland Field. Scott finished his only season with the Phillies with nine victories and 21 defeats.

102 Q. Who is the only Phillies rookie to lead the National League in runs scored?

A. Dick Allen. In 1964, the righthanded-hitting third baseman scored 125 runs, four more than runner-up Willie Mays of

The long ball—and controversy—were slugger Dick Allen's trademarks in his almost nine years with the Phillies. In 1966, he hit 40 home runs for the Phillies, the high mark of his career.

the San Francisco Giants. That season, Allen also set a National League rookie record by playing 162 games.

103 Q. *In six of the eight regular positions, the Phillies have had at least one player collect 200 or more hits in a season. Which were the two positions that haven't produced a 200-hit man?*

A. Shortstop and catcher. The most hits by a shortstop were 192 by Larry Bowa in 1978; the most by a catcher were 173 by

Spud Davis in 1933. Leaders at the other positions were first baseman Pete Rose with 208 in 1979, second baseman Dave Cash with 213 in 1975, third baseman Pinky Whitney with 207 in 1930, left fielder Lefty O'Doul with 254 in 1929, myself at center field with 221 in 1951, and right fielder Chuck Klein with 250 in 1930.

104 Q. *Who is the oldest player ever to pitch for the Phillies?*

A. Grover Alexander. He was 43 years and three months old when he pitched in nine games for the Phillies in 1930. He posted an 0 and 3 record before being released on June 3, ending his major-league career. He started three games that season, but his final appearance was in relief on May 28 at Boston's Braves Field, when he allowed two runs in the seventh and pitched a scoreless eighth inning. Harry "Socks" Seibold, the Boston Brave pitcher who won the game, 5 to 1, was the last big-league batter Alexander faced.

105 Q. *What was unusual about the game the Phillies and Cincinnati Reds played on May 30, 1895, at Philadelphia?*

A. Four Phillies batters were thrown out at first base by Cincinnati right fielder Dusty Miller. Batters have occasionally been thrown out at first base by outfielders in major-league games, but this is believed to be the only time *four* have been retired in that manner in one game by the same player.

106 Q. *When the Phillies lost 10 straight games in the final two weeks of the 1964 season in the slump that cost them the National League pennant, how many different pitchers lost games?*

A. Six. Jim Bunning lost the three games he started. Lefthanders Chris Short and Dennis Bennett each lost two, while Art Mahaffey, Bobby Shantz and John Boozer lost one apiece. Like Bunning, Short started three games, Bennett and Mahaffey two each.

107 Q. Which Phillies player hit three inside-the-park home runs in one season?

A. Dick Allen. In 1966, the righthanded-hitting slugger helped the Phillies win three games at Philadelphia's Connie Mack Stadium with his inside-the-park home runs. On June 2, in a 5 to 4 victory over the Chicago Cubs, Allen hit the first. His sixth homer of the season, it came with one runner on base in the seventh inning off righthanded pitcher Ferguson Jenkins. On July 2, in a 12 to 9 triumph over the Cubs, Allen hit the second. It came with the bases empty in the eighth inning off righthander Cal Koonce, for his 18th of the season. On August 1, in a 6 to 5 victory over the Houston Astros, Allen led off the 10th inning with his third and his 25th of the season off righthander Jim Owens to end the game.

108 Q. In the past 65 years, the only Phillies pitchers to win 20 or more games in one season were Robin Roberts, Chris Short, and Steve Carlton. How many pitchers in that span missed winning 20 games by just one victory?

A. Six: "Jumbo" Jim Elliott in 1931, Curt Davis in 1934, Jack Sanford in 1957, Art Mahaffey in 1962, Jim Bunning in 1964, 1965, and 1966, and Larry Christenson in 1977. All six were righthanded. In addition, Roberts came within one in 1956, and the lefthanded Short missed by one in 1968.

109 Q. What was unusual about 1896 Phillies shortstop Bill Hulen?

A. Hulen not only hit lefthanded, but also threw lefthanded, one of the few lefthanded shortstops in major-league history and the last to play regularly. A rookie in 1896, Hulen played shortstop in 73 of the 130 games the Phillies played that season. He also played two games at second base and 12 games in the outfield. That was his only season with the Phillies, but he appeared in 19 games for the Washington Senators of the National League in 1899—his only other major-league season.

110 Q. *What was unique about the 13th and last defeat Phillies pitcher Curt Simmons suffered in his first full major-league season of 1948?*

A. Although he lost the second game of the doubleheader to the New York Giants by only 3 to 0 on September 6 at Philadelphia's Connie Mack Stadium, the lefthander walked 12 batters in a game halted by darkness after seven innings.

Two of baseball's best lefthanded pitchers in the early 1950s were Curt Simmons of the Phillies and Bobby Shantz of the A's.

111 Q. *Who is the only Phillies player to hit into an unassisted triple play?*

A. Walter Holke. The Phillies switch-hitting first baseman came to bat in the fourth inning of the second game of a doubleheader at Boston's Braves Field on October 6, 1923, after second baseman Cotton Tierney had singled and had reached second base on outfielder Cliff Lee's single. Holke hit a line drive to Boston Braves shortstop Ernie Padgett, who caught the ball for the first out, stepped on second to double Tierney, then tagged Lee to complete the triple play. The Braves won, 4 to 1, in a game called because of darkness at the end of four and one-half innings—the final game of the season for both clubs. It was the fourth unassisted triple play in major-league history, and there have been only four since then.

112 Q. Which Phillies pitcher in this century won the most games in a season in which he lost none?

A. Marty Bystrom. Recalled from the Phillies American Association farm club at Oklahoma City on September 1, 1980, the 22-year-old rookie righthander started five games in a three-week span from September 10 through September 30 and won them all. Bystrom's first victory of the five was a shutout. The next best unbeaten record was George McQuillan's 4 and 0 in 1907, three of them shutouts.

113 Q. Who is the only Phillies player to bat in two game-winning runs during a World Series?

A. Mike Schmidt. In the 1980 World Series against the Kansas City Royals, the Phillies third baseman doubled home the winning run in the eighth inning of the second-game 6 to 4 victory, and singled in the first two runs in the third inning of a 4 to 1 sixth-game triumph. Other Phillies game-winning RBIs in World Series games were by right fielder Gavvy Cravath with a grounder to shortstop in the eighth inning of a 3 to 1 win in the first 1915 game; by right fielder Bake McBride with a three-run homer in the third inning of a 7 to 6 victory in the first 1980 game, and by second baseman Manny Trillo with an infield single in the ninth inning of the 4 to 3 fifth-game win in 1980.

Third baseman Mike Schmidt, who batted under .200 in his first full season with the Phillies, has developed into a superstar who won back-to-back Most Valuable Player Awards in 1980 and 1981.

114 Q. Which two pitchers struck out 16 Phillies batters in a game on two occasions?

A. Sandy Koufax and Steve Carlton. Los Angeles Dodgers lefthander Koufax did it June 22, 1959, in a 6 to 2 victory at the Los Angeles Coliseum, and May 26, 1962, in a 6 to 3 triumph at Dodger Stadium. The lefthanded Carlton did it September 20, 1967, while pitching for the St. Louis Cardinals in a game the Phillies won, 3 to 1, and May 21, 1970, in a game the Phillies won, 4 to 3, although Carlton was not the losing pitcher. Both games were played at Philadelphia's Connie Mack Stadium, and in each Carlton posted the 16 strikeouts while pitching only eight innings.

115 Q. Who was the first Phillies player to get a hit as a pinch-hitter in a World Series game?

A. Del Unser. The lefthanded-hitting outfielder-first baseman doubled home a run as a pinch-hitter in the eighth inning of the second game of the 1980 World Series against the Kansas City Royals, and doubled home a run in the ninth inning of the fifth game that year. Previous Phillies pinch-hitters Bobby Byrne and Bill Killefer in 1915, and Dick Whitman (twice), Putsy Caballero, and Stan Lopata in 1950 all failed before Unser came through in 1980.

116 Q. Who holds the Phillies club record for most consecutive games played?

A. I do. As Phillies center fielder, I played in 730 consecutive games from June 7, 1951, through September 26, 1954. A knee injury I suffered in a collision with Phillies left fielder Del Ennis in the outfield during an exhibition game in Wilmington, Delaware, prior to the 1955 season prevented me from playing in the season opener and ended my streak. I broke the record of 533 games set by Phillies first baseman Fred Luderus from 1911 through 1913. First baseman Pete Rose also surpassed the Luderus streak in 1982.

In 11 seasons as a Phillies outfielder in the post-World War II years, Del Ennis averaged better than 23 home runs and 100 runs batted in, and was a key player on the 1950 pennant-winning team.

117 Q. *Who is the youngest Phillies player ever to appear in a World Series game?*

A. Marty Bystrom. The righthanded pitcher was 22 years, two months, and three weeks old when he started the fifth game of the 1980 World Series.

118 Q. *The Phillies' Larry Bowa set the National League record for fewest errors by a shortstop in 150 or more games when he made only nine in 1972. Who holds the modern National League record for most errors by a shortstop in a season?*

A. Rudy Hulswitt. The Phillies shortstop made 81 errors in 138 games in 1903. As a team, the Phillies made 300 errors that season, a total surpassed by four other National League clubs. In contrast, the Phillies committed only 116 errors in 1972. On the three Phillies pennant-winning teams, Dave Bancroft committed 64 errors at shortstop in 1915, Granny Hamner committed 48 in 1950, and Bowa committed 17 in 1980.

119 Q. *Four pitchers have hurled no-hit games in both the American and National Leagues. Which of the four pitched one for the Phillies?*

A. Jim Bunning. The sidearming righthander pitched a no-hitter for the Detroit Tigers against the Boston Red Sox July 20, 1958, winning the first game of a doubleheader at Boston's Fenway Park, 3 to 0, then pitched a perfect game for the Phillies against the New York Mets June 21, 1964, winning the first game of a doubleheader at New York's Shea Stadium, 6 to 0.

120 Q. *How many successive one-run games did the Phillies play in their first two World Series?*

A. Seven. The Boston Red Sox won the last four games of the 1915 World Series by scores of 2 to 1, 2 to 1, 2 to 1, and 5 to 4, and the New York Yankees won the first three games of the 1950 World Series by scores of 1 to 0, 2 to 1 in 10 innings, and 3 to 2. In winning the 1980 World Series, the Phillies won the first and fifth games from the Kansas City Royals by scores of 7 to 6 and 4 to 3, and lost the third game, 4 to 3.

121 Q. *Who holds the National League record for career shutouts?*

A. Grover Alexander. The Hall of Fame righthander pitched 90 shutouts in his career which began in 1911 with the Phillies and ended in 1930, also with the Phillies. Sixty-one of his shutouts were pitched for the Phillies, 24 for the Chicago Cubs, and 5 for the St. Louis Cardinals.

122 Q. *In the five seasons from 1966 through 1970, the Phillies used five shortstops as regulars, each of whom played more than 125 games. Who were they?*

A. Starting in 1966, the five were Dick Groat, Bobby Wine, Roberto Pena, Don Money, and Larry Bowa. Bowa held the job from 1970 through 1981, then was traded with infielder Ryne Sandberg to the Chicago Cubs for shortstop Ivan DeJesus.

Don Money was the Phillies shortstop in 1969, then became a record-setting third baseman before being traded late in 1972.

123 Q. *Who are the only two players whose uniform numbers have been retired by the Phillies?*

A. Pitcher Robin Roberts and myself. Roberts, who wore No. 36, pitched for the Phillies from June 1948 through 1961, won 234 games, and led the league in victories in four of his six consecutive 20-win seasons. Playing outfield for the Phillies from 1948 through 1959, I wore No. 1, won two National League batting titles, and batted .311.

Art Mahaffey won 19 games for the seventh-place Phillies in 1962, but arm trouble that began the next year shortened his career.

124 Q. When Robin Roberts made his major-league debut for the Phillies in 1948, who was the winning pitcher?

A. Elmer Riddle. On June 18, 1948, the righthander pitched the Pittsburgh Pirates to a 2 to 0 victory over Roberts and the Phillies at Philadelphia's Shibe Park. Roberts had started his first professional baseball season with the Phillies Inter-State League farm club at Wilmington, Delaware, and was recalled after posting a 9 and 1 record with a 2.06 earned-run average. On July 23, five days after his big-league debut, Roberts won his first game, beating the Cincinnati Reds, 3 to 2, at Shibe Park. Former Phil Tommy Hughes was the losing pitcher.

125 Q. Since 1900, how many Phillies players have collected eight hits in a doubleheader?

A. Two: Baxter Jordan and myself. Jordan, who played third base and first base for the Phillies, had five singles and three doubles in 10 times at bat on June 26, 1938, as the Phillies split a doubleheader with the Cincinnati Reds at Philadelphia's Baker Bowl, winning the first game, 10 to 3, and losing the second, 8 to 5. Playing center field, I singled in eight of my 10 times at bat on May 20, 1951, as the Phillies won both ends of a doubleheader from the Pittsburgh Pirates by scores of 17 to 0 and 12 to 4 at Pittsburgh's Forbes Field.

126 Q. Which Phillies pitcher struck out the most batters in a nine-inning game?

A. Art Mahaffey. The righthander struck out 17 Chicago Cubs in the second game of a doubleheader on April 23, 1961, at Philadelphia's Connie Mack Stadium in a game the Phillies won, 6 to 0.

127 Q. Until Steve Carlton came to the Phillies in a trade with the St. Louis Cardinals before the 1972 season, Chris Short was the top lefthanded pitcher in the Phillies history. What team did Short defeat for his first major-league victory?

A. The Cincinnati Reds. Short entered the game in the eighth inning of the first game of a doubleheader at Philadelphia's Connie Mack Stadium on April 24, 1960, with the Reds leading, 5 to 2. He was removed for a pinch-hitter in the last of the eighth inning as the Phillies rallied for seven runs to win the game, 9 to 5.

128 Q. Which Phillies outfielder once went hitless in nine times at bat in one game?

A. Irish Meusel. Batting fifth in the Phillies batting order, the left fielder went 0-for-9 on July 17, 1918, against Lefty George Tyler as the Chicago Cubs defeated the Phillies, 2 to 1, in 21 innings at Chicago's Cubs Park.

129 Q. Who was the last pitcher to start both games of a doubleheader against the Phillies?

A. Don Newcombe. On September 6, 1950, at Philadelphia's Shibe Park, the Brooklyn Dodgers righthander shut out the Phillies, 2 to 0, in the first game of a twilight-night doubleheader. He also started the second game, pitched seven innings, and left for a pinch-hitter with the Phillies ahead, 2 to 0. Brooklyn scored three runs in the ninth inning to win, with reliever Dan Bankhead getting credit for the victory.

The irrepressible Tug McGraw has been an important member of the bullpen corps since joining the Phillies in 1975. His fine pitching helped the Phillies win the 1980 World Series.

130 Q. *Starting in 1974, the Phillies have stolen over 100 bases in each season. Before 1974, when was the last time the Phillies reached the 100-mark in stolen bases?*

A. In 1920. The Phillies stole 100 bases that season, but did not reach 80 in the 53 seasons in between.

131 Q. *Who is the only Phillies pitcher to be named National League Rookie of the Year?*

A. Jack Sanford. The hard-throwing righthander won the award in 1957 when he won 19 games, lost eight, and led the National League in strikeouts with 188. Five years later, Sanford was a 20-game winner for the only time in his 12-year major-league career—but that wasn't with the Phillies. Traded to the San Francisco Giants after the 1958 season, he helped the Giants win the 1962 pennant by winning 24 games and losing only seven.

132 Q. *First baseman Fred Merkle earned the nickname "Bonehead" for failing to touch second base on an apparent game-winning single, costing the New York Giants a key game and eventually the 1908 National League pennant. To whom was that nickname first applied in major-league baseball?*

A. Colonel John I. Rogers. With Alfred J. Reach, Rogers owned the Phillies from 1883 to 1902, and the co-owner was called "Bonehead" by George Stallings after he fired Stallings as the Phillies manager during the 1898 season.

133 Q. *Reliever Tug McGraw, pitching hero of the 1980 World Series for the Phillies, was traded by the New York Mets to the Phillies before the 1975 season in a six-player deal. Who else came to the Phillies with McGraw in that trade?*

A. Don Hahn and Dave Schneck. The two outfielders played a combined total of only 597 games in their major-league careers, including the nine Hahn played for the Phillies in 1975. To get McGraw and the two outfielders, the Phillies gave up catcher John Stearns, relief pitcher Mac Scarce, and outfielder-first baseman Del Unser. Before the 1979 season, Unser was re-signed by the Phillies as a free agent.

134 Q. Which Phillies manager in this century made his managerial debut with the club on opening day and lasted less than half a season?

A. Jack Coombs. The former star pitcher of the Philadelphia Athletics and Brooklyn Dodgers started the 1919 season as the Phillies' manager, but lasted for only 62 games, of which 44 were defeats. He was replaced as manager by outfielder Gavvy Cravath.

135 Q. Which major-league pitcher allowed the most home runs in one season?

A. Robin Roberts. The Phillies pitcher gave up 46 home runs in 1956, when he won 19 games. With the Phillies, the right-hander led the National League in home runs allowed in every season from 1954 through 1957, and in 1960. Roberts (who later pitched for the Baltimore Orioles, the Houston Astros, and Chicago Cubs) also holds the major-league career record for home runs allowed, giving up a total of 502 in 19 seasons.

136 Q. How many Phillies players have won National League batting championships in this century?

A. Five, winning a total of six titles. In 1910, left fielder Sherry Magee won with a .331 average; in 1929, left fielder Lefty O'Doul won with .398; in 1933, right fielder Chuck Klein won with .368; in 1947, center fielder Harry Walker won with .363 in 10 games with the St. Louis Cardinals and 130 with the Phillies. In 1955, I won with .338, and again in 1958 with .350.

137 Q. Which former Phillies outfielder was born in Hawaii?

A. Prince Henry Kauhane Oana. Born on January 22, 1908, at Waipahu, Hawaii, he joined the Phillies in 1934, and appeared in only six games. He went back to the minor leagues, returning to the big leagues in 1943 as pitcher for the Detroit Tigers.

138 Q. Which Phillies pitcher has won the most games in one season as a relief pitcher?

A. Jim Konstanty. In 1950, the 33-year-old righthander won 16 games and lost seven to play a vital role in winning the Phillies their second pennant. He was named the National League's Most Valuable Player that season, the first relief pitcher ever to win that award.

Jim Konstanty starred for the 1950 pennant-winning Phillies when he became the first relief pitcher ever to win the Most Valuable Player Award. He won 16 games and saved 22 others that year.

139 Q. Which Phillies players hit the most triples in one season in this century?

A. Elmer Flick and Sherry Magee. Right fielder Flick hit 17 triples to tie for second in the National League in 1901, and left fielder Magee also hit 17 in both 1905 and 1910, the second highest total in the league for both seasons.

140 Q. Dale Long of the Pittsburgh Pirates hit home runs in eight consecutive games to set a major-league record in 1956. Off which Phillies pitchers did he hit that streak's sixth and seventh homers?

A. Curt Simmons and Ben Flowers. On May 25, 1956, Long homered off Simmons at Philadelphia's Connie Mack Stadium in Pittsburgh's 8 to 5 victory, and the next day connected off Flowers to break the old record in a 6 to 2 Pittsburgh triumph. Two days later in Pittsburgh's Forbes Field, he homered in his eighth straight game, against the Brooklyn Dodgers.

141 Q. In the 1920s why did the Cincinnati Reds always pitch Pete Donohue against the Phillies?

A. Donohue won 20 games in a row against them. The righthanded pitcher joined the Reds in 1921, direct from Texas Christian University, and beat the Phillies on July 18 that season for his first professional victory. He beat the Phillies 19 more times in succession before the streak finally ended on August 19, 1925, at Philadelphia's Baker Bowl. That day, with the score tied, 4 to 4, in the ninth inning, Phillies outfielder Cy Williams foiled the "Williams Shift" by hitting a single off Donohue into the vacant left-field area to drive home the winning run.

142 Q. How many years did the Phillies play in the National League in this century before winning 100 games in one season?

A. Seventy-six. From 1900 through 1975, the most games the Phillies won in one season was 92 in 1964. In 1976, they won 101, and again 101 the following season. In their three pennant-winning seasons, the Phillies won 90 games in 1915, 91 in 1950, and 91 in 1980.

143 Q. What righthanded slugger didn't hit his first National League home run until he was 31 years old, then won six National League home run titles in a span of seven years while playing for the Phillies?

A. Gavvy Cravath. After playing a total of 116 games in the American League in 1908 and 1909 (for the Boston Red Sox, Chicago White Sox, and Washington Senators) and hitting just two home runs, the outfielder joined the Phillies in 1912. That season he hit 11 homers, tying for third in the National League. In the next seven years, he led the league in homers with 19 in 1913, 19 in 1914, 24 in 1915, eight in 1918, and 12 in 1919. He tied for the title with 12 in 1917, and hit 11 in 1916, one fewer than the league leader.

144 Q. *How many times have the Phillies been shut out in their opening game of the season in this century?*

A. Four. In 1902, Christy Mathewson of the New York Giants shut out the Phillies, 7 to 0, beating Cy Vorhees. In 1910, Nap Rucker of the Brooklyn Dodgers beat George McQuillan, 2 to 0. In 1933, Huck Betts of the Boston Braves beat John Berly, 2 to 0. And in 1973, Tom Seaver of the New York Mets beat Steve Carlton, 3 to 0.

145 Q. *Who was the first Phillies player to get a World Series hit?*

A. Grover Alexander. In the first game of the 1915 World Series against the Boston Red Sox, the star pitcher beat out a slow roller to third base with one out in the third inning, for the Phillies' first hit. The Phillies and Alexander won the game, 3 to 1, for their only World Series victory until 1980. Alexander played in three World Series, but that was the only hit he got in 13 times at bat.

146 Q. *A total of 43 players have played for both the Phillies and the Philadelphia Athletics. Name the only ones to play more than 500 games for both teams.*

A. Lave Cross and Monte Cross, who were not related. Lave Cross played several positions for the Phillies from 1892 through 1897, and played mainly third base for the Athletics from 1901 through 1905. Monte Cross played shortstop for the Phillies from 1898 through 1901, and was the Athletics' shortstop from 1902 through 1907.

147 Q. *In the second game of a doubleheader at Chicago's Wrigley Field on June 6, 1965, what was unusual about one of the three home runs Phillies outfielder John Callison hit?*

A. His bat broke in half. The lefthanded-hitting Callison hit a solo homer into the right-field seats in the first inning. In the third inning, he hit a solo homer over the right field wall when the barrel of the bat, which split in half, landed behind first base. In the ninth inning, he hit a two-run homer that enabled the Phillies to beat the Chicago Cubs, 10 to 9. In the first game, the Phillies won a pitcher's duel, 2 to 1.

This was the second time in his major-league career Callison hit three homers in one game. On September 27, 1964, he hit solo homers in the sixth and eighth innings and a two-run homer in the ninth as the Phillies lost, 14 to 8, to the Milwaukee Braves at Philadelphia's Connie Mack Stadium.

148 Q. *Why did Phillies catcher Jimmie Wilson have an easy time in the first game of a doubleheader on August 31, 1927?*

A. In a 13-inning, 3 to 2 loss to the Pittsburgh Pirates at Philadelphia's Baker Bowl that day, Wilson did not have a fielding chance. That is the longest game in National League history in which a catcher did not have a fielding chance.

149 Q. *What was unusual about the 1894 Phillies?*

A. Although they led the National League with a .349 batting average—the highest in major-league history—they finished in fourth place, 18 games behind first-place Baltimore. They had five of the eight leading hitters in the league, with four .400 hitters. Behind Boston's Hugh Duffy (who led the league with a .438 average) were Phillies outfielders Tuck Turner with .416, Sam Thompson with .404, Ed Delahanty with .400, and Billy Hamilton with .399. In addition, third baseman Lave Cross hit .386, and shortstop Joe Sullivan batted .352.

150 Q. *Name two Phillies pitchers who each struck out more than 250 batters in three seasons.*

A. Steve Carlton and Jim Bunning. The lefthanded Carlton

struck out a career-high 310 in 1972, and more than 250 in both 1980 and 1982. The righthanded Bunning struck out a career-high 268 in 1965, and more than 250 in both 1966 and 1967. Hall of Famer Grover Alexander struck out a career-high 241 with the Phillies in 1912, although he led the National League in strikeouts five times. Carlton led the league four times, Robin Roberts twice, with a career high of 198 in 1953, and Bunning once. Other Phillies pitchers who led the league were Earl Moore in 1910, Tom Seaton in 1913, Claude Passeau in 1939, Kirby Higbe in 1940, and Jack Sanford in 1957.

151 Q. *In the 1915 World Series, how many of the Phillies eight regulars batted over .200?*

A. Two. Shortstop Dave Bancroft batted .294, and first baseman Fred Luderus hit .438. As a team, the Phillies batted only .182 compared to .264 for the victorious Boston Red Sox, who nevertheless scored only two more runs (12 to 10) in the five-game Series.

In the 1950 World Series, when the Phillies lost four straight to the New York Yankees, the winners outhit the losers .222 to .203, although Phillies infielders Granny Hamner, Willie Jones, and Eddie Waitkus each batted .267 or better.

In the 1980 World Series, the Phillies outhit the Kansas City Royals .294 to .290, winning four of the six games. Three Phillies who appeared in every game—catcher Bob Boone, third baseman Mike Schmidt, and right fielder Bake McBride—each hit over .300.

152 Q. *Name the only National League player in this century to get 200 or more hits for five consecutive seasons.*

A. Chuck Klein. In his first full season of 1929, the Phillies right fielder got 219 hits, then followed with 250 hits in 1930, 200 in 1931, 226 in 1932, and 223 in 1933. In two of those seasons, he led the National League in hits. He led twice in doubles, three times in runs, four times in home runs, twice in runs batted in, once in batting average, and three times in slugging percentage. Klein was voted into the Hall of Fame in 1980.

153 Q. Which Phillies pitcher hurled four consecutive shutouts in his rookie season?

A. Grover Alexander. The rookie pitched seven shutouts in 1911, four within a 15-day span. The righthander blanked the Boston Braves September 7, the Brooklyn Dodgers September 13, the Cincinnati Reds September 17, and the Chicago Cubs September 21. All but the Brooklyn shutout were road games.

154 Q. Which Phillies carried these food nicknames—Apples, Beans, Buttermilk, Candy, Chicken, Cookie, Ham, Peaches, Peanuts, Pickles, Pretzels, Sugar, and Turkey?

A. Andy ("Apples") Lapihuska pitched for the Phillies in 1942 and 1943; Harry ("Beans") Kenner, pitcher, 1896; Tommy ("Buttermilk") Dowd, outfielder-infielder, 1897; John ("Candy") Callison, outfielder, 1960–1969; Nelson ("Chicken") Hawks, first baseman, 1925; Octavio ("Cookie") Rojas, infielder-outfielder, 1963-1969; Herman ("Ham") Iburg, pitcher, 1902; Herman ("Ham") Schulte, infielder, 1940; George ("Peaches") Graham, catcher, 1912; Harry ("Peanuts") Lowrey, outfielder-infielder, 1955; William ("Pickles") Dillhoefer, catcher, 1918; John ("Pretzels") Pezzullo, pitcher, 1935–36; Les ("Sugar") Sweetland, pitcher, 1927–1930; and Cecil ("Turkey") Tyson, first baseman, 1944.

155 Q. When pitcher Jim Konstanty started the first game of the 1950 World Series for the Phillies against the New York Yankees, how many previous games had he started since joining the Phillies near the end of the 1948 season?

A. None. Konstanty pitched six times in relief for the Phillies in 1948, 53 times in 1949, and 74 times in 1950 before starting against the Yankees. He lost that 1950 opener, 1 to 0, then relieved in both the third and fourth games as the Yankees defeated the Philllies in four games.

His only previous major-league starts were in 1944, when he started 12 games for the Cincinnati Reds, and in 1946, when he started one game for the Boston Braves. He made his first start for the Phillies in a National League game in 1951, when he appeared in 58 games, 57 in relief.

Cuban Cookie Rojas was the most versatile player in the history of the Phillies, playing every position during the 1960s.

156 Q. *When Lefty O'Doul batted .398 in 1929, the highest average for any Phillies player in this century, against which team did he compile his highest average?*

A. The St. Louis Cardinals. In 11 games at home and 11 games in St. Louis that season, the lefthanded-hitting batting champion hit .500 in St. Louis with 21 hits in 42 at-bats, and .429 at Philadelphia's Baker Bowl with 21 hits in 49 at-bats.

157 Q. *Where was the park that became known as Baker Bowl located in Philadelphia?*

A. Baker Bowl, the Phillies' home park from 1887 through June 1938 (originally called National League Park), was located at 15th and Huntington Streets. The third-base line was parallel to 15th Street, the first-base line was parallel to Huntington Street, and the center field corner was at Broad Street and Lehigh Avenue.

In July 1938, the club moved down Lehigh Avenue to share

Shibe Park with the Philadelphia Athletics. Shibe Park was bounded by Lehigh Avenue, 21st Street, Somerset Street, and 20th Street. The Phillies became the exclusive occupants of that park (re-named Connie Mack Stadium before the 1953 season) after the Athletics moved to Kansas City after the 1954 season. In 1971, the Phillies moved to Veterans Stadium in South Philadelphia at Broad Street and Pattison Avenue, also bounded by Packer Avenue and 7th Street.

158 Q. *What members of the Phillies 1950 pennant-winning pitching staff now coach college baseball?*

A. Robin Roberts and Bob Miller. Roberts coaches at the University of South Florida; Miller coaches at the University of Detroit. In 1950, Roberts won 20 games and Miller won 11, including his first eight decisions.

159 Q. *Name the four Phillies batters who struck out in a single inning against the Los Angeles Dodgers in 1965.*

A. Wes Covington, Tony Gonzalez, Dick Stuart, and Clay Dalrymple. Righthander Don Drysdale of the Dodgers struck them out in succession, but Covington reached first base on a passed ball by catcher John Roseboro on the third strike.

160 Q. *Which four athletes played for the Phillies and in either the National Basketball Association or its forerunner, the Basketball Association of America?*

A. Outfielder Frankie Baumholtz, pitcher Gene Conley, shortstop Dick Groat, and pitcher Ron Reed. Baumholtz played for the Phillies in 1956 and 1957, Conley pitched for the Phillies in 1959 and 1960, Groat played for the Phillies in 1966 and 1967, and Reed has pitched for the Phillies since 1976. Conley is the only one who played basketball while with the Phillies. He played for the Boston Celtics before the 1959 and 1960 baseball seasons, missing more than two weeks of National League play each year.

Power pitcher Ron Reed has been a righthanded stalwart in the bullpen since he was acquired from St. Louis late in 1975.

161 Q. Who is the only Phillies pitcher to pinch-hit a grand-slam home run?

A. "Schoolboy" Rowe. On May 2, 1943, Rowe homered with the bases full off Boston Braves righthander Al Javery in the second game of a doubleheader at Philadelphia's Shibe Park that the Phillies won, 6 to 5, after 12 innings. Only five major-league pitchers have hit grand-slam home runs as pinch-hitters in this century, and Rowe's is the most recent one in the National League. Rowe hit another home run as a pinch-hitter that season, connecting in the second game of a July 4 doubleheader, as the Phillies lost to the Chicago Cubs, 4 to 2, at Shibe Park.

162 Q. Which Phillies shortstop reported a bribe offer that resulted in an opposing player and coach being expelled from baseball for life?

A. Heinie Sand. In 1924, the New York Giants were battling the Brooklyn Dodgers for the National League pennant. On September 27, prior to a doubleheader in New York's Polo Grounds between the Phillies and the Giants, young New York outfielder Jimmy O'Connell offered Sand $500 "if you don't bear down too hard." Sand told his manager, Art Fletcher, about the conversation. The Giants clinched the pennant that day, but three days before the start of the World Series, Commissioner Kenesaw M. Landis banned O'Connell from baseball for life along with Giants Coach "Cozy" Dolan.

163 Q. How many men who played with the Phillies in this century later managed major-league, pennant-winning teams?

A. Ten. The list is headed by Casey Stengel, who played for the Phillies in 1920 and 1921, and managed 10 pennant-winning New York Yankee teams (1949 to 1953, 1955 to 1958, 1960). Sparky Anderson, 1959 Phillies, managed four Cincinnati Reds pennant-winners (1970, 1972, 1975, and 1976). Hughie Jennings, 1901 and 1902 Phillies, managed three Detroit Tigers pennant-winners (1907 through 1909). Pat Moran, 1910 to 1914 Phillies, managed 1915 Phillies and 1919 Cincinnati Reds pennant-winners. Danny Murtaugh, 1941 to 1943 and 1946 Phillies, managed 1960 and 1970 Pittsburgh Pirates pennant-winners. Al Dark, 1960 Phillies, managed 1962 San Francisco Giants and 1974 Oakland Athletics pennant-winners. Fred Mitchell, 1903 to 1904 Phillies, managed the pennant-winning 1918 Chicago Cubs. Darrell Johnson, 1961 Phillies, managed the pennant-winning 1975 Boston Red Sox; Dallas Green, 1960 to 1964 and 1967 Phillies, managed the pennant-winning 1980 Phillies; and Harvey Kuenn, 1966 Phillies, managed the pennant-winning 1982 Milwaukee Brewers.

164 Q. What's the record for runs batted in by a Phillies third baseman in one season?

A. One hundred and twenty-four. In 1932, Pinky Whitney batted in 124 while playing 151 games at third base. Mike Schmidt is second with 121 RBIs in 1980. Schmidt led the National League in RBIs in 1980, but Whitney's total was third in 1932.

165 Q. *Pitcher Clise Dudley of the Brooklyn Dodgers is the first major-league player to hit the first pitch thrown to him for a home run. Who threw the pitch?*

A. Claude Willoughby of the Phillies, in a game played on April 27, 1929, at Brooklyn's Ebbets Field. Despite the left-handed-hitting Dudley's homer off the righthanded pitcher, Willoughby and the Phillies defeated the Dodgers, 8 to 3.

166 Q. *Who are the only two major-league players to hit four home runs in 10-inning games?*

A. Chuck Klein and Mike Schmidt. Phillies right fielder Klein hit four homers on July 10, 1936, at Pittsburgh's Forbes Field as the Phillies beat the Pittsburgh Pirates, 9 to 6. Phillies third baseman Schmidt hit four in succession on April 17, 1976, at Chicago's Wrigley Field as the Phillies beat the Chicago Cubs, 18 to 16, after trailing 12 to 1 and 13 to 2, tying the National League record for comebacks. Both Klein and Schmidt hit their fourth homers in the 10th inning, providing the winning runs.

167 Q. *After Dick Sisler's three-run homer in the final inning of the final game at Brooklyn won the 1950 pennant for the Phillies, how many at-bats did it take him to get a World Series hit?*

A. Twelve. Sisler went 0-for-4 in the first 1950 World Series game against the New York Yankees, 0-for-5 in the 10-inning second game, and 0-for-2 in the third game before he singled over the shortstop in the sixth inning to score Del Ennis from second base, tying the score at 1 to 1. It was Sisler's only hit and only RBI in his 17 times at bat in the World Series, which the Yankees won in four straight games.

168 Q. *What is the most common surname of Phillies players in the club's history?*

A. Miller. Twelve Phillies players have been named Miller, starting with pitcher Cyclone Miller in 1884 through pitcher Stu Miller in 1956.

In 1966, Chris Short became only the second lefthanded pitcher in the modern history of the Phillies to win 20 or more games.

169 Q. Which Phillies players starred in the first regular season major-league game played indoors?

A. Pitcher Chris Short and third baseman Dick Allen. On April 12, 1965, opening night in Houston's Astrodome, Short pitched a four-hitter, and Allen hit a two-run home run off Houston Astros pitcher Bob Bruce in the third inning. The Phillies won the game, 2 to 0.

170 Q. Of the club-record 402 home runs given up by pitcher Robin Roberts in his 14 seasons with the Phillies, how many came with the bases loaded?

A. Three: one in his second season, 1949, one in 1951, and

one in 1955. Roberts gave up 258 of the 402 homers with the bases empty, 108 with one runner on base, and 33 with two men on base. Only 185 were hit in the righthander's home park. His highest one-season home total was 22 in 1957.

171 Q. *In which years did the Phillies double their attendance from the previous season?*

A. In 1905, 1915, 1943, 1946, and 1971. In 1904, the Phillies home attendance was 140,771 and jumped to 317,932 in 1905; in 1914, it was 138,474 and 449,898 in 1915; in 1942, it was 230,183 and 466,975 in 1943; in 1945, it was 310,389 and 1,045,247 in 1946, the first time in club history that home attendance topped 516,000; and in 1970, it was 708,247 and 1,511,223 in 1971. The all-time Phillies attendance record of 2,775,011 was set in 1979, when the club finished fourth in the Eastern Division.

172 Q. *Who was the most recent Phillies pitcher to hurl a complete game in a World Series?*

A. Robin Roberts. He went the route but lost to the New York Yankees, 2 to 1, in the second game of the 1950 World Series at Philadelphia's Shibe Park on a 10th-inning home run by Joe DiMaggio. In the third and fourth games of that World Series, starters Ken Heintzelman and Bob Miller were relieved. In the 1980 World Series against the Kansas City Royals, starters Bob Walk, Dick Ruthven, Larry Christenson, Marty Bystrom, and Steve Carlton—the winning pitcher in the sixth and final game—all required relief help.

173 Q. *What is the highest number of errors the Phillies have made behind a pitcher who hurled a no-hit game?*

A. Four. On September 18, 1903, Chick Fraser pitched a no-hit, no-run game against the Chicago Cubs at Chicago's West Side Grounds despite five walks and three errors by shortstop Rudy Hulswitt and one by second baseman Bill Hallman. The Phillies pounded out 14 hits off Peaches Graham and Clarence Currie to win, 10 to 0.

174 Q. *When did the Phillies first go south for spring training?*

A. In 1886. Harry Wright, who managed the Phillies from 1884 through 1893, took the club to Charleston, South Carolina, for spring training. Although the Phillies dropped one spot into fourth place in 1886, the Phillies finished with a better record, 14 games over .500 (after finishing only two games over .500 in 1885).

175 Q. *Name the only year in which the top three National League players in runs-batted-in came from the same team.*

A. In 1932. That season, first baseman Don Hurst of the Phillies led the league with 143, right fielder Chuck Klein was second with 137, and third baseman Pinky Whitney was third with 124.

176 Q. *Give the Phillies' record for wins, losses and ties in season openers during this century.*

A. When the Phillies lost their 1982 opener to the New York Mets, their record for season openers was 40 victories, 41 defeats, and two ties, starting with a victory in Boston in 1900. The ties came in 1923, in a 5 to 5, 14-inning deadlock against the Brooklyn Dodgers at Brooklyn's Ebbets Field, and in 1924, in a 6 to 6 deadlock in 11 innings against the Boston Braves at Philadelphia's Baker Bowl.

177 Q. *When Steve Carlton set an all-time Phillies record by winning 15 consecutive games in 1972, who was his starting catcher in most of those games?*

A. John Bateman, who caught the last 13 of the 15 straight victories. The hefty catcher was obtained from the Montreal Expos in a trade for catcher Tim McCarver on June 14, 1972. The following January, the Phillies released Bateman, ending his major-league career.

178 Q. *How did pitcher Tom Seaver almost join the Phillies before pitching in his first professional game?*

A. Seaver signed his first pro contract in 1966 with the Atlanta Braves, but the contract was voided because it was signed after the season began at the University of Southern California, where Seaver was a student and a member of the college's baseball team. The other 19 major-league teams were invited to participate in a drawing for the rights to Seaver, with the proviso that they would match the $40,000 bonus the Braves had paid for the collegian. Only the Cleveland Indians, the New York Mets, and the Phillies agreed to the conditions. The names of the three clubs were put in a hat and Commissioner William Eckert drew the Mets.

179 Q. *What team did the Phillies replace when they entered the National League in 1883?*

A. The Worcester, Massachusetts, Brown Stockings. The Phillies took over the franchise, but that was all they got: no players on the 1882 Worcester club came to Philadelphia in the takeover.

180 Q. *Outfielder Jimmy Piersall hit the only National League home run of his career against the Phillies. Upon hitting that homer, what did he do?*

A. He ran around the bases while facing backwards, celebrating his 100th career home run. On June 23, 1963, in the first game of a doubleheader at New York's Polo Grounds, the righthanded-hitting Piersall, then in a brief stint with the New York Mets, hit a solo homer into the right field stands off pitcher Dallas Green in the fifth inning of a 5 to 0 victory for the Mets.

181 Q. *How many Phillies pitchers have won a Gold Glove Award, given to the player voted the best fielder at his position in the league?*

A. Three. Bobby Shantz won a Gold Glove in 1964, Jim Kaat in 1976 and 1977, and Steve Carlton in 1981. All three were lefthanded.

182 Q. *How many innings did the Phillies play in the 1915 World Series before making a substitution?*

A. Thirty-four. After using only nine men in each of the first three games, Oscar Dugey pinch-ran for first baseman Fred Luderus in the eighth inning of the fourth game. Until then, eight regulars and the starting pitcher batted in the same order in every game.

183 Q. *Which Phillies pitcher hit a home run in each of four straight games in which he started?*

A. Ken Brett. In 1973, the lefthanded pitcher and batter homered on June 9 in a 4 to 1 victory over the San Diego Padres, June 13 in a 16 to 3 triumph over the Los Angeles Dodgers, June 18 in a 9 to 6 win over the New York Mets, and on June 23 in a 7 to 2 victory over the Montreal Expos. The first three games were played at Philadelphia's Veterans Stadium, the fourth at Montreal's Jarry Park. Brett finished the season with 20 hits, including five doubles and four homers, and batted in 16 runs while compiling a .250 average. He won 13 games, lost nine, and had a 3.44 earned-run average in 1973, his only season with the Phillies. After that season, he was traded to the Pittsburgh Pirates for second baseman Dave Cash.

184 Q. *What was the largest season's home attendance the Phillies drew before they moved from Baker Bowl to Shibe Park in mid-season 1938?*

A. 515,365. That was the home attendance in 1916, the year after the Phillies had won their first National League pennant. In 1916, they finished in second place, two and one-half games behind the Brooklyn Dodgers.

185 Q. *Robin Roberts was a 20-game winner for six straight seasons with the Phillies. How many times did the righthander lead the National League in earned-run average?*

A. None. Since earned runs were officially tabulated starting in 1912, the only Phillies to win earned-run titles were Grover Alexander and Steve Carlton. The righthanded Alexander led in 1915 with a 1.22 ERA, in 1916 with 1.55, and in 1917 with 1.86. The lefthanded Carlton led in 1972 with 1.97. Roberts finished second in 1953 with 2.75, and was third in 1952 with 2.59, his career low ERA.

186 Q. *Who had the briefest career as a Phillies player?*

A. Mickey Harrington, an outfielder who had starred in basketball at Mississippi Southern University and was drafted by the New York Knicks. The Phillies recalled Harrington from the minors in the middle of the 1963 season. He was used as a pinch-runner on July 10 against the San Francisco Giants, but did not appear in another game before being optioned to the Phillies' Arkansas International League farm club. He never played in another big-league game.

Others who appeared in only one game without a single at-bat include Tom Maher in 1902, third baseman Joe Bennett in 1923, first baseman Terry Lyons in 1929, and outfielder Fred Van Dusen as a pinch-hitter in 1955.

Among pitchers, righthander Art Gardiner relieved in a 1923 game and gave up a walk and a hit to the only two batters he faced; and lefthander Marty Walker started a 1928 game on September 30 at Brooklyn, gave up two hits and three walks in the first inning and was removed without retiring a batter in a 5 to 1 loss.

187 Q. *Who was the first Phillies pitcher credited with a victory in the major-league All-Star Game?*

A. Ken Raffensberger. The lefthander pitched the fourth and fifth innings on July 11, 1944, and was the winner as the National League defeated the American League, 7 to 1, at Pittsburgh's Forbes Field. Raffensberger came on after starter Bucky Walters was removed for a pinch-hitter in the third inning with the American League leading, 1 to 0. After pitching two scoreless innings in which he allowed just one hit while striking out two, Raffensberger was removed for a pinch-hitter in the midst of a four-run, fifth-inning rally.

No other Phillies pitcher has ever won an All-Star Game, but two Phillies have lost the game. Lefthander Curt Simmons was the loser in the 1957 game at St. Louis; righthander Art Mahaffey lost the second 1962 game at Chicago's Wrigley Field.

Lefthander Ken Brett was on the mound for the Phillies on July 21, 1973 when home run king Hank Aaron hit No. 700 in Atlanta.

188 Q. *Who are the youngest and oldest men ever to manage the Phillies in this century?*

A. Red Dooin and Steve O'Neill. Dooin, a Phillies catcher from 1902 through 1914, was named manager prior to the 1910 season at the age of 30 years, 10 months. O'Neill, who succeeded Eddie Sawyer as manager of the Phillies on June 27, 1952, was 63 years old nine days before he was replaced as manager by Terry Moore on July 15, 1954.

189 Q. *Who set the all-time, major-league record for runs scored in one season while playing for the Phillies?*

A. Billy Hamilton. The outfielder scored 192 runs in 1894 while playing in only 129 games, setting a record that has never been seriously threatened. New York Yankees outfielder Babe Ruth set the American League record with 177 runs in 152 games in 1921. The modern National League record was set by Phillies outfielder Chuck Klein, who scored 158 runs in 156 games in 1930.

190 Q. *In 1977, the Phillies put together their longest winning streak in this century. Which pitcher won the first game in that 13-game streak, and then lost the game that ended it?*

A. Steve Carlton. The lefthander beat the San Diego Padres, 8 to 1, at Philadelphia's Veterans Stadium to start the streak on August 3, 1977, and to end the streak, lost to the Montreal Expos, 13 to 0, on August 17 at Montreal's Olympic Stadium. Carlton won three games during the two-week streak, while Larry Christenson, Jim Lonborg, and Gene Garber won two apiece; Tug McGraw, Jim Kaat, Ron Reed, and Warren Brusstar each won one.

191 Q. *When the Phillies set a modern National League record by losing 23 games in a row in 1961, they lost at least twice to every other team in the league except one. Which team didn't beat them?*

A. The Los Angeles Dodgers. In the streak, which began July

Since joining the Phillies in 1972, pitcher Steve Carlton has made standing ovations almost commonplace. Here, he acknowledges one. Lefty has been a 20-game winner five times for the Phillies.

29 with a 4 to 3 loss to the San Francisco Giants at Philadelphia's Connie Mack Stadium, the Phillies lost two games to the Giants, four to both the Cincinnati Reds and St. Louis Cardinals, six to the Pittsburgh Pirates, three to the Chicago Cubs and four to the Milwaukee Braves before beating the Braves, 7 to 4, on August 20 at Milwaukee County Stadium to end the streak. The Phillies had lost their three-game series with the Dodgers earlier in the week in which the record losing streak began, and did not face them again until more than two weeks after the losing streak ended.

192 Q. *In 1929, Phillies first baseman Frank Hurst got one hit in each of six consecutive games. What was unusual about those hits?*

A. Each was a home run. Hurst homered July 28 and 29 at Chicago, July 30 and 31 and August 1 and 2 at Pittsburgh. However, the Phillies lost both games to the Cubs, 7 to 2 and 12 to 10, and the August 1 game to the Pirates, 3 to 1. They beat the Pirates, 13 to 5, on July 30, 6 to 2, on July 31, and 2 to 0, on August 2.

193 Q. *When the Phillies set a modern National League record by losing 23 consecutive games in 1961, which of their pitchers lost the most games?*

A. Jim Owens and Chris Short. Each lost four games. Don Ferrarese, Art Mahaffey, John Buzhardt, and Frank Sullivan lost three apiece; Robin Roberts, Jack Baldschun, and Paul Brown each lost one. Buzhardt won the game before the losing streak began, beating the San Francisco Giants, 4 to 3, in the second game of a twilight-night doubleheader July 28 at Philadelphia's Connie Mack Stadium. He ended the losing streak by beating the Milwaukee Braves, 7 to 4, in the second game of a Sunday doubleheader August 20 at Milwaukee County Stadium.

194 Q. *In 1903, the Phillies set a major-league record for consecutive games postponed during a season. How many games were postponed?*

A. Nine. From August 10 through August 19 that season, two games against the Boston Braves, three against the Cincinnati Reds, three against the Chicago Cubs, and one against the St. Louis Cardinals were postponed in succession. All were scheduled to be played in Philadelphia. The American League record for consecutive postponed games is seven by three different teams.

195 Q. *Why was the afternoon of June 1, 1923, particularly frustrating for the four Phillies pitchers who worked that day?*

A. They failed to blank the New York Giants in a single inning. En route to a 22 to 5 victory at Philadelphia's Baker Bowl, the Giants scored in every inning with 4, 2, 1, 1, 5, 5, 1, 2, and 1 off Phillies righthanded pitchers Ralph Head, Pete Behan, Jesse Winters, and Jim Bishop.

196 Q. *In which season did the Phillies win their first 17 games against one opponent?*

A. 1962. That season, the Phillies beat the Houston Colt 45s at every meeting until their final game September 4 at Colt Stadium. In that game, the Colts (later re-named the Astros) won 4 to 1, as righthander Bob Bruce held the Phillies to four hits, including a home run by center fielder Don Demeter. The Colts, playing their first season as an expansion team, lost four one-run and five two-run decisions to the Phillies before winning that final game.

197 Q. *Joe Oeschger is best known, along with rival Leon Cadore, for having pitched all 26 innings in a 1 to 1 tie between the Boston Braves and Brooklyn Dodgers in 1920 in the longest major-league game ever played. What was the most unusual game Oeschger pitched for the Phillies, for whom he played from 1914 until he was traded in 1919 to the New York Giants and then to the Braves?*

A. On May 13, 1918, Oeschger gave up a walk, two hits, and three runs in the first inning, then held the St. Louis Cardinals hitless for the next nine innings in a game that ended in a 3 to 3 tie at Robison Field, St. Louis, and was called because of darkness after 10 innings.

198 Q. *What did Babe Ruth do in the final time at bat in his major-league career?*

A. He grounded out on May 30, 1935, in the first game of a doubleheader at Philadelphia's Baker Bowl. Ruth (then with the Boston Braves) grounded out to Phillies first baseman Dolf Camilli, then left the game and retired. The Phillies won, 11 to 6.

199 Q. *Total paid attendance for the five games of the 1915 World Series was 143,351. How much did each Phillies player receive for his full share?*

A. $2,520. That was the second-highest amount for a full share for a player on the losing team at that time. For the winning Boston Red Sox, each full share was worth $3,780.

200 Q. *What was each full share worth to Phillies players in 1950 when they lost the World Series to the New York Yankees?*

A. $4,081, only $1,561 more than the value of the 1915 losing full share. Each full share for the winning Yankees was worth $5,737. By 1980, things had improved markedly for the players. The world champion Phillies each received $34,693 for a full share, and each Kansas City Royal received $32,211 for a full share. Paid attendance in 1950 for the four games was 196,009, the only time since 1939 that attendance has been under 200,000. The six games in 1980 drew 324,516.

201 Q. *Who is the only player to fill all nine positions during his Phillies career?*

A. Cookie Rojas. Primarily a second baseman from 1963 through 1969, Rojas played his first game as a left fielder for the Phillies at Dodger Stadium, Los Angeles, July 26, 1963. On June 10, 1964, the Cuban played shortstop for the first time against the Pittsburgh Pirates at Philadelphia's Connie Mack Stadium, caught for the first time July 19 against the Cincinnati Reds at Cincinnati's Crosley Field, and played all three outfield positions as well as second and third base that season. On September 16, 1965, Rojas played first base for the first time, in a game against the Milwaukee Braves at Connie Mack Stadium, and on June 30, 1967, for his ninth position he pitched a scoreless inning against the San Francisco Giants at Connie Mack Stadium. Barney Friberg, who played for the Phillies from June 15, 1925 through the 1932 season, played every infield position, pitched in one game, caught in one game and played the outfield for the Phillies—but did not play all three outfield positions.

202 Q. *Which Phillies pitcher struck out the most batters in one game?*

A. Chris Short. On October 2, 1965, the lefthander struck out 18 batters in the 15 innings he pitched in a game that ended in an 18-inning scoreless tie with the New York Mets at Shea Stadium. A Saturday night game, it was halted by the New York State curfew law early Sunday morning.

203 Q. *Who batted in the only run the Phillies scored in the first major-league night game?*

A. Mickey Haslin. The shortstop singled to score catcher Al Todd in the fifth inning at Cincinnati's Redland Field May 24, 1935. Righthander Paul Derringer pitched the Cincinnati Reds to a 2 to 1 victory. The Reds scored a run in the first inning and another in the fourth off loser Joe Bowman, who left the game for a pinch-hitter in the eighth.

204 Q. *Who pinch-hit the most home runs in one season for the Phillies?*

A. Gene Freese. The infielder came within one of the major-league record by hitting five pinch home runs in 1959, and he hit them all before mid-June. The righthanded batter hit the first April 18 with the bases loaded at Cincinnati's Crosley Field to help the Phillies beat the Cincinnati Reds, 14 to 9. He hit the second April 23 at Connie Mack Stadium with one man on base in the ninth inning in a game in which the Phillies beat the Milwaukee Braves, 4 to 3. He hit the third May 11 at the Los Angeles Coliseum with no one on base in an 11 to 10 loss to the Los Angeles Dodgers. He hit the fourth May 22 with one runner on base at Connie Mack Stadium in a 10 to 5 loss to Milwaukee, and the fifth May 31 in the eighth inning of the second game of a doubleheader at Milwaukee County Stadium in a 2 to 1 loss to the Braves. Six days later, Freese became the Phillies' regular third baseman, and his other 18 homers that season were hit as a regular player.

205 Q. *How many Phillies in this century were player-managers?*

A. Eight: catcher Chief Zimmer in 1903, outfielder Hugh Duffy from 1904 through 1906, catcher Red Dooin from 1910 through 1914, outfielder Gavvy Cravath in 1919 and 1920, pitcher Kaiser Wilhelm in 1921, first baseman Stuffy McInnis in 1927, catcher Jimmie Wilson from 1934 through 1938, and Ben Chapman, who pitched and played the infield and outfield in 1945, and pitched in 1946. Only Dooin, who played in 103 games in 1910, ever appeared in 100 or more games in a season during which he was the manager.

206 Q. *Who was the first major-league pitcher to lose all 12 games he pitched in a season?*

A. Russ Miller. Pitching for the Phillies in 1928, the 28-year-old righthander posted an 0 and 12 record for the year, his last in the big leagues. He had a 1 and 1 record for the Phillies in 1927, his only other major-league season. In 1972, lefthander Ken Reynolds lost his first 12 decisions for the Phillies, but finished that season with a 2 and 15 record.

207 Q. *Who was the last Phillies player to score five runs in one game?*

A. Don Demeter. On September 12, 1961, the Phillies center fielder scored five times in a 19 to 10 victory over the Los Angeles Dodgers at Los Angeles Coliseum. In that game Demeter batted six times, walked once, singled once, hit three home runs, struck out once, and batted in seven runs. Other Phillies players who scored five runs in a game include outfielder John Titus on June 4, 1912, in a 17 to 4 victory over the Pittsburgh Pirates at Philadelphia's National League Park; outfielder Denny Sothern on June 6, 1930, in a 14 to 5 victory over the Cincinnati Reds at Philadelphia's Baker Bowl; and second baseman Lou Chiozza on April 19, 1935, in an 18 to 7 victory over the New York Giants at Baker Bowl.

208 Q. *How many different teams did the Phillies defeat in their modern club record 13-game winning streak in August, 1977?*

A. Four. They beat the San Diego Padres twice, the Los Angeles Dodgers three times, the Montreal Expos four times, and the Chicago Cubs four times. The first eight games of the streak were played at Veterans Stadium, the last five on the road. The streak began August 3 with an 8 to 1 victory over San Diego and ended August 17 with a 13 to 0 defeat at Montreal's Olympic Stadium, one night after the Phillies had beaten the Expos there, 7 to 5 , for their 13th straight victory. Following the August 17 loss, the Phillies won their next six games.

209 Q. *In which year did the Phillies collect the most hits in major-league history?*

A. In 1930. In 156 games that season, the Phillies collected 1,783 hits to break the major-league record of 1,724, set by the Detroit Tigers of the American League in 1921. Despite their record number of hits and a team batting average of .315, the 1930 Phillies won only 52 games and finished last, 40 games behind the first-place St. Louis Cardinals.

210 Q. *Hal Kelleher pitched four seasons for the Phillies with little distinction. His major-league career ended in 1938 after what particularly embarrassing experience?*

A. In the eighth inning of a May 5, 1938 game against the Chicago Cubs at Chicago's Wrigley Field, Kelleher gave up 12 runs and set a modern National League record by facing 16 batters in one inning. The Cubs beat the Phillies, 21 to 2.

211 Q. *Which Phillies player hit the longest single in the Houston Astrodome?*

A. Mike Schmidt. On June 10, 1974, the third baseman hammered a drive that hit the public address system hanging from the roof of the Astrodome, some 300 feet from home plate and more than 115 feet above the ground. Schmidt got only a single on the blow, because the ball was in play off the speaker. It was estimated that it would have traveled well over 500 feet had the ball not hit the speaker.

212 Q. When lefthander Steve Carlton set a Phillies club record by winning 15 games in a row in 1972, how many different teams did he defeat?

A. Eleven. Carlton beat every rival team at least once and defeated the San Diego Padres, Los Angeles Dodgers, New York Mets, and Montreal Expos twice each.

Ed Delahanty was one of baseball's first long-ball hitters, and a key man in the great-hitting Phillies outfields prior to 1900.

213 Q. Which Phillies player had four brothers who also played in the major leagues?

A. Ed Delahanty, the righthanded-hitting slugger who played with the Phillies in 1888 and in 1889, and from 1891 through 1901. His younger brothers Frank, Tom, Jim, and Joe were all major leaguers. Only Ed and Tom (who made his major-league debut by playing one game with the Phillies in 1894) ever played on the same team. None of the four attained the success of Ed, who was named to the Hall of Fame in 1945.

Seven other sets of brothers also played for the Phillies, the most recent being pitchers Dennis and Dave Bennett in the early 1960s.

214 Q. *In the 1915 World Series between the Phillies and the Boston Red Sox, in which two ball parks were the games played?*

A. The first, second, and fifth games were played in Baker Bowl, in North Philadelphia, and the third and fourth games were played in Braves Field in Boston's Allston section. The Braves gave the Red Sox permission to use their park because Braves Field had just been completed and had 8,000 more seats than Fenway Park, home of the Red Sox. The year before, the "Miracle Braves" had borrowed Fenway Park for the World Series in which they beat the Philadelphia Athletics four straight games in a stunning upset.

215 Q. *Who was the last Phillies player to collect four doubles in one game?*

A. Willie Jones. The third baseman had four two-base hits in a 6 to 5 loss to the Boston Braves at Boston's Braves Field April 20, 1949. Other Phillies who doubled four times in one game were outfielder Ed Delahanty in 1899, outfielder Sherry Magee in 1914, outfielder Gavvy Cravath in 1915, outfielder Denny Sothern in 1930, and shortstop Dick Bartell in 1933.

216 Q. *In what season did the Phillies opening game end in a forfeit?*

A. In 1907. Heavy snow fell the day before the April 11 season opener at New York's Polo Grounds, and snow was piled high in foul territory. Phillies righthander Frank Corridon was pitching a one-hitter for the Phillies and was leading after eight innings when fans began walking across the field and throwing snowballs. Umpire Bill Klem then forfeited the game to the Phillies.

217 Q. *Three members of the 1980 world champion Phillies—pitcher Steve Carlton, first baseman Pete Rose, and third baseman Mike Schmidt—are generally regarded as future Hall of Famers. Who wore their uniform numbers before they did?*

A. Pitcher Fred Wenz wore Carlton's No. 32 in 1971. Infielder Mike Buskey wore Rose's 14 in 1977. And outfielder Roger Freed wore Schmidt's 20 in 1971 and 1972.

218 Q. *Who is the only major-league pitcher in the last 75 years to twice pitch two complete games in one day?*

A. Grover Alexander. The Phillies righthander beat the Cincinnati Reds, 7 to 3 and 4 to 0, on September 23, 1916, at Philadelphia's Baker Bowl, and defeated the Brooklyn Dodgers, 5 to 0 and 9 to 3, September 3, 1917, at Brooklyn's Ebbets Field.

219 Q. *Which former Phillies player was born in Czechoslovakia?*

A. Elmer Valo. The hustling outfielder, who began his major-league career with the Philadelphia Athletics in 1940, was born on March 5, 1921 in Ribnik, Czechoslovakia. Playing with the A's in Philadelphia through 1954, he moved with the club to Kansas City in 1955, then was traded to the Phillies during the 1956 season. Before the 1957 season, Valo was traded to the Brooklyn Dodgers and played with several other teams before rejoining the Phillies in June 1961. He finished the season with them, then retired and later became a Phillies scout.

220 Q. *Who is the only Phillies player to strike out five times in one nine-inning game and walk five times in another?*

A. Dick Allen. The slugger struck out five times in five at-bats in the first game of a doubleheader won by the Phillies, 5 to 0, June 28, 1964, at Busch Stadium, St. Louis. Four years later, on August 16, 1968, at Philadelphia's Connie Mack Stadium, Allen walked five times in five plate appearances in a game the Phillies lost, 7 to 5, to the San Francisco Giants.

221 Q. *In which four-year span did the Phillies use five different managers?*

A. 1918 to 1921. Pat Moran managed the Phillies for the fourth year in a row in 1918; Jack Coombs and Gavvy Cravath managed in 1919; Cravath managed in 1920, and "Wild Bill" Donovan and "Kaiser" Wilhelm managed in 1921. Wilhelm lasted through the 1922 season.

222 Q. *Since the introduction of the lively ball in 1920, 11 Phillies pitchers have lost 20 or more games in one season. Which two of them are now in the Hall of Fame?*

A. Eppa Rixey and Robin Roberts. The lefthanded Rixey inducted into the Hall of Fame in 1963, posted an 11 and 22 record in 1920. The righthanded Roberts, who entered the Hall of Fame in 1976, had a 10 and 22 record in 1957. Other 20-game losers were George Smith (4 and 20 in 1921), Jack Scott (9 and 21 in 1927), Bucky Walters (11 and 21 in 1936), Hugh Mulcahy (10 and 20 in 1938 and 13 and 22 in 1940), Rube Melton (9 and 20 in 1942), Ken Raffensberger (13 and 20 in 1944), Dick Barrett (7 and 20 in 1945), Murry Dickson (10 and 20 in 1954), and Steve Carlton (13 and 20 in 1973).

223 Q. *How many Hall of Fame players started their major-league careers as Phillies?*

A. Eight. Followed by the year they first played for the Phillies and, in parentheses, the year they were inducted into the Hall of Fame, they were: Grover Alexander, 1911 (1938), shortstop Dave Bancroft, 1915 (1971), outfielder Ed Delahanty, 1888 (1945), outfielder Elmer Flick, 1898 (1963), outfielder Chuck Klein, 1928 (1980), second baseman Nap Lajoie, 1896 (1937), pitcher Eppa Rixey, 1912 (1963), and pitcher Robin Roberts, 1948 (1976).

224 Q. *How many Hall of Fame players ended their major-league playing careers as Phillies?*

A. Seven: outfielder Hugh Duffy played his last game in 1906, when he was also manager of the Phillies, and entered the Hall of Fame in 1945; outfielder Hack Wilson, 1934 (1979); outfielder Chuck Klein, 1944, when he was also a coach (1980); Jimmie Foxx, 1945, when he played first base, third base, and pitched (1951); pitcher Tim Keefe, 1893 (1964); pitcher Kid Nichols, 1906 (1949); and pitcher Grover Alexander, 1930 (1938). In addition, Harry Wright ended his 18-year managing career in 1893, his 10th season as manager of the Phillies, and was inducted in 1953.

225 Q. *Lefthanded-throwing catchers have been rare in the major leagues. Which Phillies lefthanded catcher was considered to be the best ever to play in the big leagues?*

A. Jack Clements. A 200-pound Philadelphia native, Clements played for the Phillies from 1884 through 1897, and was first-string catcher in 10 of those 14 seasons. He batted over .300 five times.

226 Q. *In 1915, 14 non-pitchers on the Phillies were eligible to play in the World Series; in both 1950 and 1980, there were 15. How many of these failed to appear in any World Series games?*

A. Six. In 1915, catcher Bert Adams and outfielder Bud Weiser were not used; in 1950, outfielder Stan Hollmig; and in 1980, infielders Ramon Aviles and John Vukovich and outfielder George Vukovich.

227 Q. *Which Phillies pitcher allowed the most hits while pitching a shutout?*

A. George Smith. On August 12, 1921, the 29-year-old right-hander blanked the Boston Braves, 4 to 0, at Boston's Braves Field, while allowing 12 hits. Smith won only three other games that season and lost 20.

228 Q. *Who was the deranged woman who shot Phillies first baseman Eddie Waitkus in a Chicago hotel room in 1949?*

A. Ruth Steinhagen. On June 14, Waitkus was seriously wounded when he was shot in the chest at the Edgewater Beach Hotel. He returned to play regularly in 1950, helping the Phillies win the pennant. Ms. Steinhagen was confined to a mental institution.

229 Q. *Who hit the first World Series home run for the Phillies?*

A. Fred Luderus. In the fourth inning of the fifth and final game of the 1915 World Series against the Boston Red Sox at Philadelphia's Baker Bowl, with one out and nobody on base,

First baseman Eddie Waitkus was shot by a deranged woman in a Chicago hotel during the 1949 season, but recovered and helped the Phillies win the National League pennant the next year.

the lefthanded-hitting first baseman hit a home run over the right field wall. The home run off pitcher Rube Foster, put the Phillies ahead, 3 to 2, and they added another run in the inning. But the Red Sox rallied to win, 5 to 4, to end the Series. It was 65 years before another Phillies player hit a World Series home run.

230 Q. *How many Phillies batters have hit over .360 in a season in this century?*

A. Three. Left fielder Lefty O'Doul batted .398 in 1929 and .383 in 1930; right fielder Chuck Klein hit .386 in 1930 and .368 in 1933, and right fielder Elmer Flick batted .378 in 1900.

231 Q. *How many Phillies pitchers have hurled complete-game shutouts in their first major-league games?*

A. Four. Eddie Stack beat the Chicago Cubs,1 to 0,on June 7, 1910,at Philadelphia's National League Park. Niles Jordan beat the Cincinnati Reds, 8 to 0, on August 26, 1951, at Philadelphia's Shibe Park. Dave Downs beat the Atlanta Braves, 3 to 0, on September 2, 1972, at Atlanta-Fulton County Stadium. And Marty Bystrom beat the New York Mets, 5 to 0, on September 10, 1980, at New York's Shea Stadium.

Stack, Downs and Bystrom were righthanded; Jordan was lefthanded. Stack finished his brief major-league career in 1914 with a 26 and 24 record for the Phillies, Brooklyn Dodgers, and Chicago Cubs. Jordan pitched for Cincinnati in 1952 before retiring with a 2 and 4 record for his major-league career. Downs finished 1972 with a 1 and 1 record and didn't pitch in the major leagues again. Bystrom is still an active pitcher.

232 Q. *Which Phillies outfielder batted .313, hit 18 home runs, knocked in 72 runs in his rookie season, but never again played in the major leagues?*

A. Buzz Arlett. The switch-hitting slugger was 32 years old as a rookie in 1931, but was a defensive liability both in the outfield and at first base. In 1932, playing with the Baltimore Orioles of the International League, Arlett hit 54 home runs.

233 Q. *What caused the most recent forfeited home game involving the Phillies?*

A. Unruly fans. On August 21, 1949, with one out in the ninth inning of the second game of a doubleheader at Philadelphia's Shibe Park, first baseman Joe Lafata of the New York Giants hit a line drive to center field. Second base umpire George Barr ruled that I, playing center field for the Phillies, had trapped the ball. Incensed by the decision, the fans littered the field with bottles, cans, and other refuse. When they continued the bombardment after being warned of a possible forfeit, the umpires forfeited the game. At the time, New York was leading, 4 to 2.

234 Q. *Who was the last Phillies player to ground into three double plays in one game?*

A. I was. On June 28, 1959, I came to bat four times in a 6 to 0 loss to the San Francisco Giants at San Francisco's Seals

Righthander Marty Bystrom was a key pitcher in the late-season stretch run as the Phillies won the 1980 pennant and World Series. He was recalled from the minor leagues on September 1.

Stadium, was walked once by lefthander Johnny Antonelli and grounded into double plays in my other three times at bat. Ironically, I rank among the 10 most difficult players to double in major-league history: in my 15-year major-league career, I grounded into only 101 double plays.

235 Q. *When the Phillies won their first National League pennant in 1915, how many different players did they use?*

A. Twenty-three. The Phillies used nine pitchers (including George McQuillan, obtained from the Pittsburgh Pirates during the season), three catchers, six infielders, and five outfielders. By contrast, in 1915, the Philadelphia Athletics—American League champions the season before—used 56 different players, still the major-league record. They finished last, 58½ games behind the first-place Boston Red Sox. The 1950 pennant-winning Phillies used 32 players, including 15 pitchers, and the 1980 world champion Phillies used 39 players, 17 of them pitchers.

236 Q. *Among Phillies pitchers in the last 80 years, who collected the most hits in one season?*

A. "Schoolboy" Rowe. In 1943, the big righthander pounded out 36 hits in 120 times at bat for a .300 average in his first season with the Phillies. Fifteen of his 36 hits came as a pinch-hitter in 49 at-bats, both of those totals leading National League pinch-hitters. Of Rowe's 36 hits, 25 were singles, seven were doubles, and four were home runs. He batted in 18 runs, scored 14, and drew 15 walks. The Phillies finished seventh that season, and Rowe was the club's best pitcher, with 14 victories and eight defeats.

237 Q. *Who was the first Phillies player to serve as a designated hitter in a non-exhibition game?*

A. Greg Luzinski. In the opening game of the 1980 World Series against the Kansas City Royals, Luzinski batted fifth as the designated hitter and went hitless as the Phillies won, 7 to 6. Keith Moreland and Lonnie Smith were also used as designated hitters later in the World Series—which uses the designated hitter in even years.

238 Q. *How many Phillies players have hit two home runs in the opening game of a season?*

A. Four: Sherry Magee in 1914, Lefty O'Doul in 1929, Chuck Klein in 1931, and Don Money in 1969. All were outfielders except Money, who was the Phillies regular shortstop that season.

239 Q. *Which Phillies player appeared in the most games in a season without hitting a home run?*

A. Larry Bowa. The shortstop played in 159 games in 1971 and failed to hit a home run in 650 official times at bat. The major-league record for homerless at-bats is held by Pittsburgh

Pirate shortstop "Rabbit" Maranville, who had 672 in 1922. In addition to 1971, Bowa had 500 at-bats in three other seasons in which he failed to hit a home run.

240 Q. Which Phillies pitcher earned the nickname "The Giant-Killer" in 1908?

A. Harry Coveleski. A rookie lefthander from Shamokin, Pennsylvania, Coveleski beat the New York Giants three times in five days in the final 10 days of the season, costing the Giants the pennant. At the end of the season, New York lost the replay of a September 23 tie game with the Chicago Cubs, giving the Cubs the pennant. Coveleski had a 1 and 0 record in a brief stint with the Phillies in 1907, then was brought up at the end of the 1908 season after posting a 22 and 15 record for

Left fielder Greg Luzinski heard a great many cheers in his decade with the Phillies, during which his slugging helped win four division titles and the 1980 pennant and World Series.

Lancaster of the Tri-State League. For the Phillies in 1908, he made five starts, winning four, losing one, and completing all five. His first victory over the Giants was by a 7 to 0 score September 29. He also beat the New Yorkers, 6 to 3, on October 1, and 3 to 2, on October 3. The Cubs won the pennant-deciding game by a 4 to 2 score on October 8 at New York's Polo Grounds.

241 Q. *How many innings was the longest game in Phillies history?*

A. Twenty-one. On July 17, 1918, the Chicago Cubs beat the Phillies, 2 to 1, in 21 innings at Cubs Park. The longest game *won* by the Phillies was a 20-inning, 5 to 4 victory over the Atlanta Braves at Philadelphia's Veterans Stadium May 4, 1973. (The Phillies had lost a 20-inning game, 2 to 1, to the Cubs August 24, 1905, at Philadelphia's National League Park, and played a 9 to 9 tie in 20 innings with the Brooklyn Dodgers April 30, 1919, at Philadelphia's Baker Bowl.)

242 Q. *Which pitcher was traded by the Phillies, then pitched a no-hit, no-run game in his debut with his new team?*

A. Don Cardwell. With first baseman Ed Bouchee, the righthander was traded by the Phillies to the Chicago Cubs for second baseman Tony Taylor and catcher Cal Neeman on May 13, 1960. On May 15, Cardwell pitched a no-hitter to defeat the St. Louis Cardinals, 4 to 0, in the second game of a doubleheader at Chicago's Wrigley Field.

243 Q. *Who was the last Phillies pitcher to hurl a complete game in post-season play?*

A. Steve Carlton. He went the full nine innings to beat the Los Angeles Dodgers, 9 to 4, in the third game of the 1978 National League Championship Series on October 6 at Dodger Stadium. In the fourth and final game of that series, in the five Championship Series games against the Houston Astros in 1980, and in the six World Series games that season, the Phillies starting pitcher failed to go the distance.

Catcher Andy Seminick was a block of granite behind the plate, and a slugger who helped the Phillies win the pennant in 1950.

244 Q. How many Phillies players have hit three home runs in one game?

A. Twelve. Right fielder John Manning was the first to do it in 1884. The others were catcher Butch Henline in 1922, center fielder Cy Williams in 1923, left fielder Johnny Moore in 1936, catcher Andy Seminick in 1949, catcher Del Wilber in 1951, left fielder Del Ennis in 1955, right fielder Don Demeter in 1961, right fielder John Callison in 1964 and again in 1965, left fielder Dick Allen in 1968, first baseman Deron Johnson in 1971, and third baseman Mike Schmidt in 1979. Three Phillies players, including Schmidt, hit four in one game.

245 Q. *Who were the winning pitchers in the last game at Connie Mack Stadium in 1970, and the first game at Veterans Stadium in 1971?*

A. Dick Selma and Jim Bunning. Selma relieved Barry Lersch in the ninth inning and was the winning pitcher when the Phillies beat the Montreal Expos in 10 innings, 2 to 1, October 1, 1970. Bunning beat the Expos, 6 to 1, in the opening game of the season April 10, 1971.

246 Q. *In 1935, the Phillies lost the first night game in major-league history at Cincinnati. How did they do in their first night game at home?*

A. They lost to the Pittsburgh Pirates, 5 to 2, at Shibe Park, on June 1, 1939. The Phillies played seven night games at home that season and lost the first four before defeating the Brooklyn Dodgers, 3 to 2, on August 8, with Hugh Mulcahy posting the victory.

247 Q. *How many different Phillies scored in the club's 26 to 23 loss to the Chicago Cubs at Chicago's Cubs Park on August 25, 1922?*

A. Thirteen. Every Phillies starting player except pitcher Jimmy Ring scored at least once; the substitute first baseman, shortstop, catcher, center fielder, and pitcher also scored. Nine Cubs scored, each at least twice.

248 Q. *There have been 17 no-hit games pitched against the Phillies in this century. Which pitcher came closest to pitching a perfect game?*

A. George ("Hooks") Wiltse. The New York Giants lefthander retired the first 26 Phillies batters in order in the morning game July 4, 1908, at New York's Polo Grounds, but then hit opposing pitcher George McQuillan on the arm with a 2 and 2 pitch. The Giants won the game, 1 to 0, in the 10th inning, and McQuillan was the only batter to reach base against Wiltse.

On August 18, 1960, Milwaukee Braves righthander Lew

Burdette beat the Phillies, 1 to 0, in Milwaukee County Stadium. The only Phillies batter to reach base was outfielder Tony Gonzalez, hit on the right shoulder by a 1 and 1 pitch with one out in the fifth inning. He was later erased in a double play.

On June 4, 1964, Los Angeles Dodger lefthander Sandy Koufax beat the Phillies, 3 to 0, at Philadelphia's Connie Mack Stadium. The only Phillies batter to reach base was Dick Allen, who walked with two out in the fourth inning.

249 Q. *The Phillies are the only National League team to win three 18 to 0 games in this century. Name the winning pitchers in these shutouts.*

A. George McQuillan, Claude Willoughby, and Roy Hansen. McQuillan beat the Pittsburgh Pirates at Pittsburgh's Forbes Field on July 11, 1910. Willoughby won over the Cincinnati Reds in the first game of a doubleheader at Cincinnati's Redland Field on August 10, 1930; and Hansen blanked Cincinnati at Philadelphia's Baker Bowl on July 14, 1934.

Other lopsided Phillies shutout victories include Russ Meyer's 17 to 0 triumph over Pittsburgh in 1951, Chris Short's 16 to 0 victory over Houston in 1963, Alex Ferguson's 15 to 0 win over Boston in 1928, and Bucky Walters' 15 to 0 triumph over New York in 1936. The most lopsided shutout pitched *against* the Phillies since 1900 was Pat Malone's 16 to 0 victory for the Chicago Cubs on May 4, 1929, in the first game of a doubleheader at Philadelphia's Baker Bowl.

250 Q. *Which Phillies pitcher has hit the most home runs in one season?*

A. Rick Wise. The righthander hit six home runs in 1971; twice that season, he hit two in one game. The first time was June 23 at Cincinnati's Riverfront Stadium when he not only hit two home runs, but also pitched a no-hitter to beat the Cincinnati Reds, 4 to 0. The second time he hit two homers in a game was August 28 in the second game of a twilight-night doubleheader at Philadelphia's Veterans Stadium to help the Phillies beat the San Francisco Giants, 7 to 3. The six home runs he hit that season exceeded by one his major-league career total up to that time.

251 Q. *In each of the three World Series the Phillies have played, one Phillies regular batted over .400. Who were the players?*

A. In 1915, first baseman Fred Luderus batted .438. Shortstop Granny Hamner batted .429 in 1950, and catcher Bob Boone batted .412 in 1980.

252 Q. *Only six players have ever collected 250 or more hits in a season. Who were the only two who were teammates?*

A. Lefty O'Doul and Chuck Klein of the Phillies. In 1929, Phillies left fielder O'Doul set a National League record with 254 hits; in 1930 right fielder Klein had 250 hits. In 1930, O'Doul's record for hits was tied by Bill Terry, first baseman for the New York Giants. Only George Sisler of the St. Louis Browns ever collected more in one season, getting 257 in 1920. The other 250-hit men were Al Simmons of the 1925 Philadelphia Athletics, with 253, and Rogers Hornsby of the St. Louis Cardinals, with 250 in 1922.

253 Q. *How many changes were made in the playing rules because of plays involving the Phillies during one week of the 1966 season?*

A. Two. On July 4, in the first game of a doubleheader with the New York Mets at Philadelphia's Connie Mack Stadium, Phillies first baseman Bill White lifted a high pop foul to the left of the plate. Mets catcher Jerry Grote went into the Phillies dugout and was ready to make the catch when Phillies Manager Gene Mauch hit him across the arms, causing him to drop the ball. Because Grote had invaded the dugout, Mauch's action was legal. After the season, the rule was changed to require opposing players to vacate any space needed by defensive players to make a play.

On July 8 at Wrigley Field, Chicago Cubs outfielder Billy Williams lifted a high pop fly near third base. Phillies third baseman Dick Allen bumped into Cubs base-runner Ron Campbell, who was standing on the bag, and the ball fell untouched. Williams was called out because of Campbell's interference. After the season, the rule was amended so that a player who is simply standing on a base can't be considered as interfering with a fielder trying to field a batted ball.

254 Q. *Who hit the most doubles in one season for the Phillies?*

A. Chuck Klein. In 1930, the right fielder hit 59 doubles to lead the National League and break the club record of 55, set by Ed Delahanty in 1899. Klein also hit 50 doubles in 1932 to finish second in the league. Shortstop Dick Bartell had 48 in 1932, and no other Phillies player in this century has had more than 46.

255 Q. *Since 1900, how many Phillies managers never played in a major-league game?*

A. Six. From 1899 through 1902, Billy Shettsline, who had never played professional baseball, managed the Phillies. The others who never played major-league baseball were Billy Murray, manager from 1907 through 1909; Eddie Sawyer, manager from July 26, 1948 through June 26, 1952, and from July 22, 1958 through April 12, 1960; Frank Lucchesi, from 1970 through July 9, 1972; Paul Owens, from July 10, 1972 through the end of that season; and Danny Ozark, who managed from 1972 through August 30, 1979.

256 Q. *Only four Phillies players have reached base 300 or more times on hits and walks in a season. Who's the only one to do it twice?*

A. I am. As center fielder, I had 175 hits and 125 walks in 1954, and 215 hits and 97 walks in 1958, when I won my second National League batting title. Other Phillies players to reach base 300 or more times in a season were center fielder Billy Hamilton, with 220 hits and 126 walks in 1894; and left fielder Lefty O'Doul, with 254 hits and 76 walks in 1929, and right fielder Chuck Klein, with 250 hits and 54 walks in 1930.

257 Q. *Which Phillies pitcher won the most shutouts in season openers?*

A. Chris Short. The lefthander pitched a shutout on April 12, 1965, against the Houston Astros in the Astrodome, another on April 10, 1968, against the Los Angeles Dodgers in Dodger Stadium, and a third April 7, 1970, against the Chicago Cubs at Philadelphia's Connie Mack Stadium. All were 2 to 0 victories.

Other Phillies who pitched opening game shutouts were Kid Gleason over New York, 4 to 0, in 1890; Frank Corridon over New York, 3 to 0, in 1907; Earl Moore over New York, 2 to 0, in 1911; Tom Seaton over Brooklyn, 1 to 0, in 1913; Grover Alexander over Boston, 3 to 0, in 1915; Les Sweetland over Brooklyn, 1 to 0, in 1930; Ken Heintzelman over Boston, 4 to 0, in 1949.

258 Q. *What is the earliest date in a season on which the Phillies have played a National League game?*

A. April 6. On that date, the Phillies lost, 3 to 2, at Pittsburgh in 1971; lost at New York, 3 to 0, in 1973; defeated New York, 5 to 4, in 1974, and lost, 8 to 1, at St. Louis in 1979.

259 Q. *How many Phillies players have committed more than one error in a World Series?*

A. None. In 1915, first baseman Fred Luderus, shortstop Dave Bancroft and catcher Ed Burns each committed one error against the Boston Red Sox. In 1950, second baseman Mike Goliat, third baseman Willie Jones, shortstop Granny Hamner, and Andy Seminick each committed one against the New York Yankees. In 1980, second baseman Manny Trillo and pitcher Larry Christenson each committed one error against the Kansas City Royals.

260 Q. *How long did John Quinn serve as general manager of the Phillies?*

A. Thirteen and one-half years. Quinn, general manager of the Boston Braves when they won the National League pennant in 1948, and general manager of the Milwaukee Braves when they won the 1957 and 1958 pennants, was hired early in 1959 as the Phillies general manager, succeeding H. Roy Hamey, who resigned to return to the New York Yankees. Quinn served until he was replaced by Paul Owens on June 3, 1972. Quinn's father Bob had been a long-time major-league executive, and Quinn's sons, Jack and Bob, were also baseball executives. His son-in-law, Roland Hemond, has been general manager of the Chicago White Sox since 1973.

261 Q. *The Phillies were the first major-league team to have four players get 200 or more hits in a season. Who were the players, and what was the year?*

A. In 1929, Lefty O'Doul, Chuck Klein, Fresco Thompson, and Pinky Whitney all produced 200 or more hits. Left fielder O'Doul set a National League record with 254 hits; right fielder Klein had 219, second baseman Thompson had 202, and third baseman Whitney had 200. The only other major-league team to have four players slug 200 hits or more in a season was the 1937 Detroit Tigers, with outfielders Gee Walker (213) and

First baseman Fred Luderus played 10 years for the Phillies and helped them win their first pennant in 1915. In the World Series against the Boston Red Sox, he hit his team's only homer.

Pete Fox (208), first baseman Hank Greenberg (200), and second baseman Charley Gehringer (209).

262 Q. What teams played the first tie game in National League history?

A. Philadelphia and Louisville played 14 innings to a 2 to 2 tie on May 25, 1876.

263 Q. Who was the first baseball player to enter military service in the Second World War?

Popular Frank Lucchesi managed in the minor leagues for 19 years before taking over the Phillies in 1970. Here, he waits for a relief pitcher to take over for lefthander Ken Reynolds (number 47).

A. Pitcher Hugh Mulcahy. Before entering the service, he had won 40 games and lost 76 for the Phillies in the four previous seasons, earning the nickname "Losing Pitcher." Drafted into the Army March 6, 1941, he missed almost five full seasons. He returned late in 1945 in time to appear in five games, but was never again a regular starter.

264 Q. On August 28, 1952, Phillies pitcher Robin Roberts started a streak of 28 straight complete games that didn't end until July 9, 1953. What team finally knocked Roberts out of the box?

A. The Brooklyn Dodgers. Roberts was replaced in the top of the eighth inning, when the Dodgers scored two runs to take a 5 to 4 lead over the Phillies at Philadelphia's Connie Mack Stadium. Bob Miller relieved with one out and retired the side, then was replaced in the home eighth by pinch-hitter Smoky Burgess, who doubled home the tying and winning runs as the Phillies won, 6 to 5. In his complete game streak, Roberts won his last eight starts in 1952, then won 13 and lost six and tied one in his first 20 starts in 1953. Half of his six losses were to Brooklyn.

265 Q. Which Phillies player collected the most hits in World Series play during his career?

A. Larry Bowa. The Phillies shortstop had nine hits in the six games against the Kansas City Royals in the 1980 World Series. First baseman Fred Luderus had seven hits in the five-game Series against the Boston Red Sox in 1915, and shortstop Granny Hamner had six hits in the four-game Series against the New York Yankees in 1950. Third baseman Mike Schmidt had eight hits in the 1980 Series.

266 Q. Who are the only two major-league players to hit grand-slam home runs as pinch-hitters in both the American and National Leagues?

A. Jimmie Foxx and Roy Sievers. Both righthanded sluggers hit their National League pinch-hit grand slams while with the Phillies. Foxx hit his Phillies grand slam May 18, 1945, in an 11 to 8 loss to the St. Louis Cardinals at Philadelphia's Shibe Park.

Larry Bowa was the most consistent fielding shortstop in the major leagues during his years (1970-1981) with the Phillies.

Sievers hit his for the Phillies May 26, 1963, in a 10 to 4 victory over the Cincinnati Reds at Cincinnati's Crosley Field. Foxx hit his American League grand slam for the Philadelphia Athletics September 21, 1931, and Sievers hit his American League grand slam for the Chicago White Sox on June 21, 1961.

267 Q. *Which Phillies player hit the most home runs in one month?*

A. Cy Williams. The lanky center fielder hit 15 home runs in May, 1923. That's still the National League record for that month.

268 Q. *Which players hit the two most important home runs in Phillies history?*

A. Dick Sisler and Mike Schmidt. Sisler hit a three-run homer in the 10th inning of the final game of the 1950 season at

Dick Sisler will be remembered as long as baseball is played in Philadelphia. His dramatic, 10th-inning home run on the last day of the season in Brooklyn gave the Phillies the 1950 pennant.

Brooklyn's Ebbets Field on October 1 to give the Phillies a 4 to 1 victory and the National League pennant by one game. Sisler, a lefthanded batter, hit his homer off Dodgers righthander Don Newcombe into the left-field stands. Schmidt hit a two-run homer on Oct. 4, the next-to-last day of the 1980 season, at Montreal's Olympic Stadium in the 11th inning to give the Phillies a 6 to 4 victory and the National League's Eastern Division title. The righthanded-hitting Schmidt hit his homer off Expos righthander Stan Bahnsen into the left-field stands. The Phillies then beat the Houston Astros in the five-game Championship Series to clinch the pennant, and defeated the Kansas City Royals in six games to win their first World Series title. Sisler's home run was his 13th of the season; Schmidt's was his 48th.

269 Q. *Which Phillies pitchers have appeared in more than 70 games in one season?*

A. Jim Konstanty, Jack Baldschun, Dick Selma, and Gene Garber. Konstanty was in 74 games in 1950, Baldschun in 71 games in 1964, Selma in 73 in 1970, and Garber in 71 in 1975. All four were righthanders who pitched only in relief in the seasons listed, and all but Konstanty had a losing season in that year. Konstanty won 16 games, lost seven, saved 22 and was named the National League's Most Valuable Player as the Phillies won the 1950 pennant. Baldschun had a 6 and 9 record with 21 saves in 1964, Selma an 8 and 9 record with 22 saves in 1970, and Garber a 10 and 12 record with 14 saves in 1975.

270 Q. *Which famous slugger, eventually elected to the Hall of Fame, pitched the Phillies to his only career victory in his final big-league season?*

A. Jimmie Foxx. The husky Maryland native, who played most of his 20-year, major-league career as a first baseman and hit 534 home runs, pitched in nine games for the Phillies in 1945, posting the only mound victory of his career when he started and beat the Cincinnati Reds, 4 to 2, in the second game of a doubleheader August 19 at Philadelphia's Shibe Park. The losing pitcher was Howie Fox.

271 Q. *Who were the only two major-league club presidents barred from baseball for life in this century?*

A. Horace Fogel and William D. Cox, both Phillies presidents. Fogel, a former Philadelphia sportswriter, served as club president from late 1909 through the 1912 season. He was barred by the other seven owners at a post-season hearing after he had

Bobby Wine was a strong-armed shortstop for the Phillies in the 1960s and has been a coach with the club for the last decade.

charged that the umpires and National League President Thomas Lynch had plotted to guarantee the 1912 pennant to the New York Giants. Cox, who headed a group that bought the Phillies in February 1943, after the league had taken over the franchise, was barred after the 1943 season by Commissioner Kenesaw M. Landis for betting on Phillies games. The club was then purchased by Robert R. M. Carpenter in November 1943.

272 Q. *Who were the Phillies coaches whose three teams won the National League pennant?*

A. In 1915, Manager Pat Moran handled the club by himself. In 1950, Manager Eddie Sawyer had Benny Bengough, Dusty Cooke, George Earnshaw, and Cy Perkins as coaches. In 1980, Ruben Amaro, Billy DeMars, Lee Elia, Mike Ryan, Herm Starrette, and Bobby Wine served as coaches under Manager Dallas Green.

273 Q. *In the highest-scoring season opener in the Phillies' history, how many runs did they score?*

A. Nineteen. The Phillies held a 17 to 8 lead going into the ninth inning at Boston's Congress Street Grounds on April 19, 1900, but the Boston Braves (then known as the Beaneaters) scored nine runs to tie the score. The Phillies scored twice in the 10th inning to win the game, 19 to 17, as the two teams set a major-league record for the most runs ever scored in a season's opener.
    Other high-scoring Phillies openers include a 12 to 7 loss to Brooklyn in 1901, a 15 to 7 loss to New York in 1927, a 13 to 5 victory over New York in 1932, a 12 to 3 loss to Brooklyn in 1935, a 12 to 5 loss to Brooklyn in 1938, and a 12 to 4 victory over Cincinnati in 1962.

274 Q. *Who pitched the most season-openers in the history of the Phillies?*

A. Robin Roberts. The righthander pitched every opening game from 1950 through 1961, winning five, losing six, and having one no-decision start in 1958 at Cincinnati when the

Phillies rallied to win, 5 to 4, with rookie righthander Ray Semproch credited with his first big-league victory after three innings of relief work.

275 Q. *Since the Phillies moved into Veterans Stadium in 1971 for regular-season games, what are the largest and smallest crowds they have had?*

A. 63,346 and 4,149. On August 10, 1979 for a twilight-night doubleheader with the Pittsburgh Pirates, the Phillies drew their largest crowd. On May 6, 1974, for a Monday night game against the San Diego Padres, the Phillies drew their smallest crowd. The largest crowd ever to see a Pennsylvania baseball game was 65,838 on October 21, 1980, when the Phillies won the sixth and final game of the 1980 World Series.

276 Q. *In the fastest nine-inning game in major-league history, who were the opposing pitchers?*

A. Lee Meadows of the Phillies and Jesse Barnes of the New York Giants. At New York's Polo Grounds on September 28, 1919, Barnes pitched the Giants to a 6 to 1 victory over the Phillies in the first game of a doubleheader that lasted only 51 minutes. It was the 25th victory of the season for Barnes, the 20th loss of the year for Meadows.

277 Q. *Which pitcher who spent seven and one-half seasons with the Phillies holds the National League record for the most 1 to 0 shutouts won?*

A. Grover Alexander. The righthander won 17 shutouts by 1 to 0 scores. The major-league record of 38 is held by Walter Johnson of the Washington Senators. In 1913, 1916, and 1917, Alexander tied for the National League lead in 1 to 0 shutouts won while pitching for the Phillies.

278 Q. *Who is the only Phillies player to get six hits in a game in this century?*

A. Connie Ryan. The second baseman collected two doubles and four singles in six times at bat in a game the Phillies lost,

16 to 14, on April 16, 1953 at Pittsburgh's Forbes Field. Before 1900, four other Philadelphia players got six hits in a game: shortstop Davy Force (the first major leaguer to do it) in 1876, first baseman Jack Boyle in 1893, and outfielders Ed Delahanty and Sam Thompson in 1894.

279 Q. *Ten major-league players have hit four home runs in one game. How many of the seven National Leaguers to do it were Phillies?*

A. Three. Outfielder Ed Delahanty hit four home runs at Chicago's West Side Grounds on July 13, 1896. Outfielder Chuck Klein did it at Pittsburgh's Forbes Field in a 10-inning game July 10, 1936. And third baseman Mike Schmidt did it at Chicago's Wrigley Field in a 10-inning game April 17, 1976.

The other major leaguers to hit four in National League games were Bobby Lowe of Boston in 1894, Gil Hodges of Brooklyn in 1950, Joe Adcock of Milwaukee in 1954, and Willie Mays of San Francisco in 1961. The three American Leaguers to do it were Lou Gehrig of the New York Yankees in 1932, Pat Seerey of Chicago in 1948, and Rocky Colavito of Cleveland in 1959. Six of the players who hit four homers in a game were outfielders, three were first basemen, and one was a third baseman.

280 Q. *Since the introduction of the lively ball in 1920, which Phillies player hit more home runs in one season than the rest of his team combined?*

A. Cy Williams. In 1927, the Phillies right fielder hit 30 homers to tie for the National League home-run crown. The rest of the Phillies hit only 27 homers. Two years later, the Phillies hit 153 homers to lead the league.

281 Q. *What major-league record did St. Louis Cardinals hitters tie against the Phillies in 1922?*

A. Most consecutive hits in one inning. On June 12, 1922, at Philadelphia's Baker Bowl, the Cardinals got 10 hits in a row in the sixth inning en route to a 14 to 8 victory in which they collected 23 hits off pitchers Lee Meadows, Jesse Winters, and Jimmy Ring. In the sixth inning, Jack Fournier, Milt Stock, Eddie Ainsmith, Doc Lavan, "Specs" Torporcer, Max Flack, Jack Smith, Rogers Hornsby, Austin McHenry, and Fournier, up for the second time, all hit safely in succession. Seven runs were scored, but the Cardinals would have scored more had not Torporcer, after hitting a ball out of the park, passed Lavan. He was declared out for passing his teammate and credited with only a single.

282 Q. *Who was the last Phillies player to hit for the cycle (single, double, triple, and home run) in a nine-inning game?*

A. John Callison. The lefthanded-hitting right fielder came to bat six times at Pittsburgh's Forbes Field in a 13 to 4 Phillies victory over the Pittsburgh Pirates on June 27, 1963, and walked, singled, doubled, tripled, hit a three-run home run and batted in four runs. Phillies outfielders Cy Williams and Chuck Klein both hit for the cycle twice in their careers.

Tony Gonzalez (left) and John Callison, who were regular outfielders for the Phillies in the 1960s, get together in the 1970s before an Old-Timers Game at Philadelphia's Veterans Stadium.

283 Q. *What Phillies player batted in the most runs during one game?*

A. Russ Wrightstone. At Philadelphia's Baker Bowl on June 11, 1926, the Phillies infielder batted in nine runs in a 13 to 11 victory over the Pittsburgh Pirates. Four members of the Phillies—first baseman Kitty Bransfield in 1910, outfielder Gavvy Cravath in 1915, third baseman Willie Jones in 1958, and third baseman Mike Schmidt in 1976—each batted in eight runs in one game.

284 Q. *What are the most runs batted in by a rival player against the Phillies?*

A. Eight. Five different players have done so in a game against the Phillies: Dave Robertson of the Pittsburgh Pirates in 1921, Mel Ott of the New York Giants in 1936, Alex Campouris of the Cincinnati Reds in 1937, Ed Bailey of the Chicago Cubs in 1965, and Chris Speier of the Montreal Expos in 1982. The first three games were played at Philadelphia's Baker Bowl, the fourth at Chicago's Wrigley Field, and the fifth at Montreal's Olympic Stadium.

285 Q. *Who is the only player to lead both major leagues in total bases for four straight seasons in the last 70 years?*

A. Chuck Klein. The Phillies right fielder led in total bases with 445 in 1930, 347 in 1931, 420 in 1932, and 365 in 1933.
   The only other major leaguer to lead both leagues four years in a row was Pittsburgh Pirates shortstop Honus Wagner, who led from 1906 through 1909, with a high of 308 in 1908. Klein's 1930 total is the fourth highest in major-league history.

286 Q. *What is the highest total of home runs hit in one month by Phillies third baseman Mike Schmidt?*

A. Fourteen. In June 1977, the righthanded-hitting slugger hit 14 home runs and batted in 28 runs. His other monthly highs through the 1982 season are 11 in April 1976, 12 in May 1970, 13 in July 1979, 12 in August 1975, nine in September 1980, and four in October 1980.

287 Q. *Which rookie was called up from the minor leagues in the final month of the season and became the third member of the Phillies to hit a home run in his first major-league time at bat?*

A. Ed Sanicki. The righthanded-hitting outfielder hit 33 home runs for the Phillies International League farm club at Toronto in 1949 before being recalled by the Phillies. On September 14 at Pittsburgh's Forbes Field, he entered the game as a defensive replacement in right field, came to bat for the first time in the ninth inning with two runners on base and hit a home run off pitcher Rip Sewell to help the Phillies win, 12 to 4. On September 19 at Sportsman's Park, St. Louis, Sanicki hit a two-run homer off lefthander Howie Pollet in a 4 to 3 Phillies' victory over the St. Louis Cardinals. And on September 28 at Philadelphia's Shibe Park he hit a home run off Sheldon Jones to help the Phillies beat the New York Giants, 2 to 0. The homers were Sanicki's only hits in 13 times at bat in the seven games he played with the Phillies that season. His only other major-league experience was in 1951 when he appeared in 13 games with the Phillies, collecting a single and a double in four times at bat.

288 Q. *What major-league home run record was set June 17, 1876?*

A. A player hit two home runs in one game for the first time in major-league history. George Hall, the Philadelphia left fielder, hit them. He hit three other home runs that season to lead the National League with five.

289 Q. *Five teams in this century have lost three consecutive 1 to 0 games, but the Phillies are the only major-league team to suffer three straight 1 to 0 losses in the last 65 years. In what year?*

A. In 1960. During that season, the Phillies lost to the San Francisco Giants, 1 to 0, May 11 at San Francisco's Candlestick Park, and bowed, by the same score, to the Giants the next afternoon. The next night at Cincinnati's Crosley Field, the Phillies lost to the Cincinnati Reds, 1 to 0. The Phillies collected only two hits in each of the games at San Francisco, and got seven at Cincinnati. In the first inning of the next game,

May 14 at Cincinnati, the Phillies ended a streak of 29 consecutive scoreless innings on a home run by rookie Tony Curry. Curry hit a two-run homer in the third inning to help the Phillies beat Cincinnati, 5 to 2.

The other National League teams that lost three 1 to 0 games were the Brooklyn Dodgers in 1908 and the Pittsburgh Pirates in 1977. The American League teams were the St. Louis Browns and the Washington Senators, both in 1909.

290 Q. *Which Phillies relief pitcher posted three victories in three consecutive games?*

A. Gene Garber. On May 15, 1975, Garber was the winning pitcher as the Phillies beat the Cincinnati Reds, 5 to 3, in the second game of a twilight-night doubleheader at Philadelphia's Veterans Stadium. The next night, Garber won again as the Phillies beat the Atlanta Braves, 12 to 8, at the Vet, and the following night, May 17, Garber was the winner again as the Phillies beat the Braves, 9 to 8.

291 Q. *What was unusual about a six-game series the Phillies played against the New York Giants in June 1929?*

A. The Giants scored 73 runs and won every game, scoring at least 11 runs in each game. The series, played at Philadelphia's Baker Bowl, opened with a June 19 doubleheader which the Giants won, 15 to 14 in 11 innings and 12 to 6 in nine. The Giants won, 11 to 6 on June 20, 11 to 5 on June 21, then took a Saturday doubleheader on June 22, 12 to 6 and 12 to 5. The only pitcher to have two decisions in the series was Phillies righthander Ray Benge, who lost the first and sixth games for two of his 15 defeats against 11 victories that season.

292 Q. *When the Phillies lost the most one-sided shutout in major-league history, how many pitchers did they employ?*

A. One. On August 21, 1883, at Providence, Rhode Island, the Providence Grays beat the Phillies, 28 to 0, pounding pitcher Art Hagan for 26 hits in the eight innings in which they batted. Hagan committed 11 of the Phillies' 27 errors. (Prior to 1888, walks, wild pitches, and passed balls were all charged as errors.)

293 Q. *What major-league record did Phillies infielder Davy Johnson set in 1978?*

A. Two grand-slam home runs by a pinch-hitter in the same season. The righthanded-hitting Johnson hit his first with the score tied in the fifth inning on April 30 to help the Phillies defeat the San Diego Padres, 11 to 4. He hit his second with none out in the ninth inning June 3 to give the Phillies a 5 to 1 victory. Both grand-slam homers were hit at Philadelphia's Veterans Stadium.

294 Q. *What freak accident doomed any pennant hopes the Phillies had in 1953?*

A. While cutting the grass at his home on June 3, pitcher Curt Simmons cut off part of his left big toe with a power mower. The lefthander did not start another game for a month.

295 Q. *Which Phillies outfielder ended the longest, consecutive-scoreless-inning streak by a pitcher in major-league history?*

A. Howie Bedell. On June 8, 1968, at Dodger Stadium, Los Angeles, Los Angeles Dodgers righthander Don Drysdale had pitched 58 ⅔ straight scoreless innings when Bedell, batting for pitcher Larry Jackson, hit a sacrifice fly to left field to score Tony Taylor from third base in the fifth inning. The Dodgers and Drysdale beat the Phillies, 5 to 3.

296 Q. *The Phillies' longest winning streak in this century is 13 games. What is their longest all-time winning streak?*

A. Sixteen. In 1887, 1890 and 1892, the Phillies won 16 straight games. The 1887 streak began September 15, included a tie game October 7, and extended through October 8. The

1890 streak started July 8 and lasted until July 26 and included a 10 to 8 victory in 15 innings on July 22. The 1892 streak began June 10 and lasted through June 28.

297 Q. *What team ended the longest, consecutive-scoreless-inning streak ever compiled by a Phillies pitcher?*

A. The St. Louis Cardinals. Phillies rookie Grover Alexander pitched shutouts for the Phillies in 1911 on September 7 at Chicago, September 13 against Brooklyn, September 17 at Cincinnati, and September 21 at Chicago. On September 24 at Robison Field, St. Louis, the Cardinals scored in the sixth inning to end the streak after 41 innings.

298 Q. *What team scored the most runs in a game against the Phillies in this century?*

A. The St. Louis Cardinals. On July 6, 1929, at Philadelphia's Baker Bowl, the Cards beat the Phillies, 28 to 6, scoring 10 runs in the first inning and 10 runs in the fifth. Outfielder Chick Hafey and first baseman Jim Bottomley hit grand-slam home runs.

299 Q. *What is the record for errorless innings played in one game by the Phillies?*

A. Twenty. On July 17, 1918, at Chicago's Cubs Park, the Cubs beat the Phillies, 2 to 1 in 21 innings, scoring with none out in the final inning. The Cubs also went errorless, setting a National League record that still stands.

300 Q. *What was unusual about the last game pitcher Charley Stanceu won in his career for the Phillies?*

A. The righthander ended a record streak of victories by the Brooklyn Dodgers at Philadelphia's Shibe Park in 1946. On August 11 in the first game of a doubleheader, the Phillies and Stanceu beat the Dodgers, 7 to 6, to end a streak of 18 consecutive victories for the Dodgers in Philadelphia. The streak began with a 10 to 1 decision May 5, 1945, in the first game of a doubleheader. In the two games prior to the August 11 doubleheader, the Dodgers shut out the Phillies, 1 to 0 and 6 to 0. The Phillies also won the second game of the August 11 doubleheader, 6 to 4. Stanceu, obtained from the New York Yankees earlier in that season, won only two games and lost four in his final major-league season that year.

301 Q. *Which pitcher who finished his major-league career with the Phillies had unusual success against the New York Mets?*

A. Larry Jackson. The righthander, who pitched for the Phillies from 1966 through 1968 and for the St. Louis Cardinals and Chicago Cubs earlier in his career, won his first 18 decisions with the Mets. On June 20, 1967, Jackson pitched a 4 to 0 victory over New York in which he allowed only one hit, a second-inning double by Tommy Davis, for his sixth shutout against the Mets. The streak ended August 14 when Jack Fisher and the Mets beat Jackson and the Phillies, 8 to 3. Both these games were played at Philadelphia's Connie Mack Stadium. Fisher made a habit of ending opposing streaks against the Mets: he ended a 12 and 0 streak by Pittsburgh Pirates righthander Bob Friend in 1964, and a 19 and 0 streak by San Francisco Giants righthander Juan Marichal in 1967.

302 Q. *Which Phillies pitchers defeated a rival team at least seven times in one season?*

A. Grover Alexander, Bill Duggleby, and Tom Seaton. Alexander had an 8 and 0 record against the Cincinnati Reds in 1916. Duggleby had a 7 and 0 record against the Boston Braves in 1906, and Seaton had a 7 and 1 record against the Braves in 1913. Duggleby's record in 1906 against the Chicago Cubs, however, was almost the opposite, with two victories and seven defeats.

303 Q. *Which former Phillies player holds the club record for games played, times at bat, and hits?*

A. I do. In my 12 seasons with the Phillies, 1948 through 1959, I played in 1,794 games, had 7,122 at-bats, and 2,217

St. Louis Cardinals star Stan Musial and I were two of the premier National League hitters in the post-World War II era. Musial won seven batting crowns, and I won two.

hits. Shortstop Larry Bowa, who played with the Phillies from 1970 through 1981, is second in games with 1,739, second in at-bats with 6,815, and fourth in hits with 1,798. Ed Delahanty, who played for the Phillies in 1888 and 1889 and from 1891 through 1901, leads in runs with 1,365, doubles with 432, triples with 151, and runs batted in with 1,286.

304 Q. *In 1973, pitcher Steve Carlton was a 20-game loser for the Phillies, but in what season did the lefthander get off to his worst start since joining the Phillies in 1972?*

A. In 1982. That year, Carlton lost his first four decisions before starting a three-game winning streak and going on to win 23 games for the sixth time in his career, five times for the Phillies. In 1973, Carlton won two of his first three decisions and four of his first six, but finished with a 13 and 20 record.

305 Q. What is the best home record the Phillies have recorded?

A. Sixty victories, 21 defeats in 1977.

306 Q. Which Los Angeles Dodgers pitcher was a streaky winner and loser against the Phillies in the 1960s?

A. Don Drysdale. Starting June 25, 1959, when he pitched the Dodgers to a 5 to 2 victory at the Los Angeles Coliseum, the big righthander beat the Phillies 13 straight times through June 1, 1962, when he pitched the Dodgers to an 8 to 5 victory in the second game of a twilight-night doubleheader at Philadelphia's Connie Mack Stadium. In his next decision with the Phillies on May 14, 1963 at Dodger Stadium, the Phillies ended Drysdale's streak with a 5 to 1 victory. That was the first of nine consecutive decisions over Drysdale by the Phillies. That streak lasted until August 27, 1965, when Drysdale and the Dodgers edged the Phillies, 9 to 8, at Connie Mack Stadium.

307 Q. Who holds the Phillies club record for pinch-hits in one season?

A. Greg Gross. In 1982, the Phillies outfielder-first baseman collected 19 hits in 53 times at bat for a .358 average as a pinch-hitter. His 19 pinch-hits broke the club record of 18, first set by Rene Monteagudo, a lefthanded-hitting outfielder-pitcher who was 18-for-52 as a pinch-hitter for the Phillies in 1945, and tied by lefthanded-hitting outfielder-first baseman Dave Philley, who was 18-for-44 as a pinch-hitter in 1958. Philley set a major-league record that season by collecting eight pinch-hits in succession. Monteagudo, Philley, and the lefthanded-hitting Gross all led the National League in their record years.

308 Q. How many times in this century has the Phillies pitching staff led the National League in strikeouts?

A. Twice. In 1913, the 14 pitchers used by the Phillies led with 667 strikeouts. And in 1982, the 16 pitchers used by the Phillies led with 1,002 strikeouts.

309 Q. *Who holds the National League record for the most consecutive errorless games and the most consecutive errorless chances accepted by a second baseman in a season?*

A. Manny Trillo. The Phillies second baseman set both records in 1982. He played in 89 straight games without an error from April 9 through July 30, and accepted 497 straight chances without an error from April 9 until the sixth inning on July 31 in a game against the Chicago Cubs at Veterans Stadium.

During his four seasons with the Phillies, second baseman Manny Trillo was a record-setting fielder and a fine clutch hitter.

310 Q. *What National League player has had the most consecutive-game hitting streaks of 20 or more games?*

A. Pete Rose. The Phillies first baseman hit in 21 straight games in 1982, the seventh time in his career he has had a hitting streak of 20 or more games, tying the major-league record set by Ty Cobb in the American League.

311 Q. *Why are the dates of June 10, 1981, and August 10, 1981, important to Phillies fans?*

A. Those are the dates of the games in which Phillies first baseman Pete Rose tied and broke Stan Musial's National League record for most base-hits in a career. The June 10 game was the last one played by the Phillies before the strike by the players, and the August 10 game was the first played by the Phillies after the strike ended. His record-tying hit was off Nolan Ryan of the Houston Astros, and his record-breaking hit was an eighth-inning single off Mark Littell of the St. Louis Cardinals. Both games were played at Philadelphia's Veterans Stadium.

312 Q. *On what day of the week have the Phillies won the fewest games in their long history?*

A. On Sundays. Because of Pennsylvania's Blue Laws, no Sunday games were played in the state until the 1934 season. The Phillies played their first home Sunday game on April 29, 1934, losing to the Brooklyn Dodgers, 8 to 7. They didn't win their first home Sunday game until May 20 when they defeated the Pittsburgh Pirates, 16 to 4, with a potent offense and the pitching of Curt Davis.

Nobody has ever played the game harder than Pete Rose, safe at third base here against Montreal. Rose joined the Phillies in 1979, and broke the National League record for total hits in 1981.

Index

Aaron, Hank, 35
Adams, Bert, 226
Adams, Bobby, 31
Adcock, Joe, 279
Ainsmith, Eddie, 281
Alexander, Grover Cleveland, 10, 22, 50, 61, 73, 80, 86, 104, 121, 145, 150, 153, 185, 218, 223, 224, 257, 277, 297, 302
Allen, Dick, 25, 102, 107, 169, 220, 244, 248, 253
All-Star Game, 15, 25, 187
Amaro, Ruben, 85, 272
American League record, 189, 194
Anaheim Stadium, 25
Anderson, Sparky, 163
Antonelli, Johnny, 234
Arkansas farm club, 186
Arlett, Buzz, 232
Ashburn, Richie, 21, 49, 51, 58, 83, 103, 116, 123, 125, 136, 233, 234, 256, 303
Astrodome (Houston), 169, 211, 257
Atlanta Braves, 35, 88, 178, 231, 241, 290
Atlanta-Fulton County Stadium, 35, 231
Attendance, 171, 184, 275
Augusta, GA, 4
Aviles, Ramon, 226

Bahnsen, Stan, 268
Bailey, Ed, 284
Baker Bowl (Philadelphia), 5, 46, 48, 84, 125, 141, 148, 156, 157, 176, 184, 195, 198, 207, 214, 218, 229, 241, 249, 281, 283, 284, 291, 298
Baldschun, Jack, 193, 269
Baltimore, 94, 149
Baltimore Orioles, 135
Bancroft, Dave, 118, 151, 223, 259
Bankhead, Dan, 129
Barnes, Jesse, 276
Barr, George, 233
Barrett, Dick, 222
Barry, Jack, 100
Bartell, Dick, 215, 254
Basketball Association of America, 160
Bateman, John, 177
Batters,
 averages of, 6, 136, 149, 151, 156, 230, 251
 championship, 51, 136, 256
 consecutive hits by, 27, 281
 designated hitter as, 237
 doubles by, 215, 254
 game-winning RBIs by, 113
 grand-slam home runs by, 41, 42, 67, 161, 266, 293
 grounding into double play by, 234
 hitless, 128
 hits by, 27, 40, 99, 103, 125, 152, 192, 209, 252, 256,
  261, 278, 278, 281
 consecutive game, 64, 310
 doubleheader, 125
 one month totals for, 40
 one season totals for, 209
 hitting for cycle by, 282
 home runs by, 7, 8, 11, 29, 46, 56, 66, 75, 84, 92, 143, 147, 166, 169, 192, 238, 244, 268, 279, 280, 288, 293
  first at bat, 48, 68, 287
  inside the park, 107
  most games without, 239
  one month totals for, 267, 286
 pinch-hitting by, 17, 25, 43, 115, 161, 204, 236, 266, 293, 307
 pitchers as, 46, 75, 183, 236, 250
 rookie, 48, 68, 232
 runs by, 72, 102, 189, 207, 247, 273, 298
 runs batted in by, 100, 113, 164, 175, 203, 283, 284
 singles by, 83, 211
 strikeouts by, 114, 159, 220
 times reaching base by, 30, 256
 total bases by, 285
 triples by, 139
 walks by, 220
 winning runs by, 69
Baumholtz, Frankie, 160
Bedell, Howie, 295
Behan, Pete, 195
Belinsky, Bo, 35
Benge, Ray, 37, 291
Bengough, Benny, 272
Bennett, Dave, 231
Bennett, Dennis, 106, 231
Bennett, Joe, 186
Berly, John, 144
Betts, Huck, 144
Bicknell, Charlie, 29
Biloxi, MI, 4
Binghamton (NY) North High School, 28
Birmingham, AL, 4
Bishop, Jim, 195
Blue Jays, 3
Bonds, Bobby, 68
"Bonehead," 132
Bonura, Zeke, 29
Boone, Bob, 151, 251
Boozer, John, 85, 106
Boston, 1, 89, 249, 257, 279
Boston Beaneaters, 273
Boston Braves, 5, 66, 80, 104, 111, 144, 153, 155, 176, 194, 197, 198, 215, 227, 260, 273, 302
Boston Bruins, 32
Boston Celtics, 160
Boston Red Sox, 23, 84, 100, 119, 120, 143, 145, 151, 163, 199, 214, 229, 235, 259, 265
Bottomley, Jim, 298
Bouchee, Ed, 242
Boudreau, Lou, 23

Bowa, Larry, 103, 118, 122, 239, 265, 303
Bowman, Joe, 203
Boyle, Jack, 278
Bradenton, FL, 4
Bransfield, Kitty, 283
Braves Field (Boston), 104, 111, 214, 215, 227
Brazle, Al, 21
Bresnahan, Roger, 79
Brett, Ken, 35, 183
Brooklyn, 257, 273, 279, 297
Brooklyn Dodgers, 33, 48, 81, 129, 134, 140, 144, 153, 162, 165, 176, 184, 186, 197, 218, 219, 231, 241, 246, 264, 268, 289, 300, 312
Brown, Paul, 193
Bruce, Bob, 169, 196
Brusstar, Warren, 190
Buffalo, 14
Buffinton, Charlie, 89
Bunning, Jim, 2, 7, 20, 36, 106, 108, 119, 150, 245
Burdette, Lew, 248
Burgess, Smoky, 264
Burns, Ed, 259
Busch Stadium (St. Louis), 14, 43, 56, 220
Buskey, Mike, 217
Buzhardt, John, 193
Byrne, Bobby, 115
Bystrom, Marty, 112, 117, 172, 231

Caballero, Putsy, 12, 115
Cadore, Leon, 197
Callison, John, 25, 87, 147, 154, 244, 282
Camilli, Dolf, 198
Campbell, Ron, 253
Campouris, Alex, 284
Campbell, Ron, 253
Candlestick Park (San Francisco), 38, 47, 68, 289
Cardwell, Don, 242
Carey, Max, 49
Carlton, Steve, 2, 22, 50, 59, 78, 88, 108, 114, 127, 144, 150, 172, 177, 181, 185, 190, 212, 217, 222, 243, 304
Carpenter family, 3, 13
Carpenter, Robert R.M., 13, 271
Carroll, Clay, 66
Cash, Dave, 99, 103, 183
Catchers, 6, 8, 19, 70, 79, 82, 94, 103, 148, 177, 225
Cepeda, Orlando, 44
Chance, Frank, 45
Chapman, Ben, 60, 205
Charleston, SC, 4, 174
Charlotte, NC, 4
Chicago, 297
Chicago Cubs, 23, 33, 50, 62, 76, 80, 93, 107, 121, 122, 126, 128, 135, 147, 153, 161, 163, 166, 173, 191, 192, 194, 208, 210, 231,

240, 241, 242, 247, 249, 253, 257, 284, 299, 301, 302, 309
Chicago White Sox, 15, 143, 260, 266, 279
Chiozza, Lou, 207
Christenson, Larry, 46, 108, 172, 190, 259
Cincinnati, 246, 273, 274, 289, 297
Cincinnati Reds, 5, 8, 10, 17, 31, 41, 46, 52, 66, 72, 75, 81, 85, 101, 105, 124, 125, 127, 141, 153, 155, 163, 191, 194, 201, 203, 204, 207, 218, 231, 249, 250, 266, 270, 284, 289, 290, 302
Clark, Watty, 69
Clearwater, FL, 4
Clements, Jack, 82, 225
Cleveland, 279
Cleveland Indians, 23, 66, 77, 178
Cobb, Ty, 310
Colavito, Rocky, 279
Coleman, John, 1
Collins, Phil, 46
Colts Stadium (Houston), 85, 196
Comiskey Park (Chicago), 15
Concepcion, Dave, 66
Congress Street Grounds (Boston), 273
Conley, Gene, 160
Connie Mack Stadium (Philadelphia), 5, 31, 35, 53, 56, 72, 75, 76, 93, 98, 107, 110, 114, 126, 127, 140, 147, 157, 191, 193, 201, 204, 220, 245, 248, 253, 257, 264, 301, 306
Cooke, Dusty, 272
Coombs, Jack, 60, 134, 221
Corridon, Frank, 216, 257
Coveleski, Harry, 240
Covington, Wes, 159
Cox, William D., 271
Cravath, Gavvy, 60, 113, 134, 143, 205, 215, 221, 283
Crosley Field (Cincinnati), 41, 56, 85, 201, 204, 226, 289
Cross, Lave, 146, 149
Cross, Monte, 146
Cubs Park (Chicago), 33, 128, 241, 247, 299
Culver, George, 81
Currie, Clarence, 173
Curry, Tony, 289
"The Curveless Wonder," 63
Czechoslovakia, 219

Dalrymple, Clay, 38, 85, 159
Dark, Al, 98, 163
Davis, Curt, 108, 312
Davis, Spud, 6, 103
Davis, Tommy, 301
DeJesus, Ivan, 122
Delahanty, Ed, 27, 64, 149, 213, 215, 223, 254, 278, 279, 303
Delahanty, Frank, 213
Delahanty, Jim, 213

Delahanty, Joe, 213
Delahanty, Tom, 213
DeMars, Billy, 272
Demeter, Don, 87, 196, 207, 244
Dernier, Bob, 45
Derringer, Paul, 203
Detroit Tigers, 32, 119, 137, 209, 261
Dickson, Murry, 222
Dillhoefer, Pickles, 154
DiMaggio, Joe, 172
DiMaggio, Vince, 67
Dobernic, Jess, 75
Dodger Stadium (Los Angeles), 114, 201, 243, 257, 295, 306
Dolan, Cozy, 162
Donohue, Pete, 141
Donovan, "Wild Bill," 60, 221
Dooin, Red, 70, 79, 188, 205
Dowd, Tommy, 154
Downs, Dave, 231
Drysdale, Don, 159, 295, 306
Dudley, Clise, 165
Duffy, Hugh, 149, 205, 224
Dugey, Oscar, 182
Duggleby, Bill, 68, 302
Dusak, Erv, 29

Earnshaw, George, 272
Eastern League, 28
Ebbets Field (Brooklyn), 9, 69, 80, 165, 176, 186, 218, 268
Eckert, William, 178
Edgewater Beach Hotel, 228
Elia, Lee, 272
Elliott, Jumbo Jim, 108
Ennis, Del, 75, 116, 167, 244
Essegian, Chuck, 17

Farrell, Dick, 53
Fenway Park (Boston), 119, 214
Ferguson, Alex, 249
Ferguson, Bob, 60
Ferguson, Charlie, 16, 22, 89
Ferrarese, Don, 193
Ferrell, Wes, 66
Fielding,
 chances, 49, 148
 consecutive errorless, 309
 errorless innings, 299
 errors, 87, 118, 173, 259
 games, consecutive errorless, 309
 Gold Glove Award, 181
 percentage, 54
 putouts, 54
 triple plays, 21, 85, 111
Fillingim, Dana, 24
First basemen, 19, 99, 103, 192, 229
Fisher, Jack, 301
Fitzsimmons, Fred, 60
Flack, Max, 281
Fletcher, Art, 162
Flick, Elmer, 139, 223, 230
Flowers, Ben, 140
Fogel, Horace, 3, 13, 271
Forbes Field (Pittsburgh), 56, 125, 140, 166, 187, 278, 279, 282, 287
Force, Davy, 278

Foster, Rube, 84, 229
Fournier, Jack, 281
Fox, Howie, 270
Fox, Pete, 261
Foxx, Jimmie, 224, 266, 270
Fraser, Chick, 71, 173
Freed, Roger, 66, 217
Freese, Gene, 204
Friberg, Barney, 201
Friend, Bob, 7, 301

Gainesville, FL, 4
Garagiola, Joe, 21
Garber, Gene, 190, 269, 290
Gardiner, Art, 186
Gehrig, Lou, 279
Gehringer, Charley, 261
"The Giant-Killer," 240
Giles, Bill, 13
Glasses, 18
Glaviano, Tommy, 21
Gleason, Kid, 22, 257
Goliat, Mike, 259
Gonzalez, Tony, 87, 159, 248
Graham, Peaches, 154, 173
Green, Dallas, 41, 42, 60, 74, 163, 180, 272
Greenberg, Hank, 261
Grimsley, Ross, 66
Groat, Dick, 122, 160
Gross, Greg, 307
Grote, Jerry, 85, 253

Hafey, Chick, 298
Hagan, Art, 292
Hahn, Don, 133
Hall, George, 288
Hallman, Bill, 173
Hall of Fame, 9, 222, 223, 224, 270
Hamey, H. Roy, 260
Hamilton, Billy, 51, 64, 149, 189, 256
Hamner, Granny, 21, 75, 77, 118, 151, 251, 259, 265
Hansen, Roy, 249
Harrington, Mickey, 186
Harris, Bucky, 60
Haslin, Mickey, 203
Hawaii, 137
Hawks, Nelson, 154
Head, Ralph, 195
Hebner, Richie, 32
Heintzelman, Ken, 172, 257
Hemond, Roland, 260
Henline, Butch, 244
Herrnstein, John, 62, 85
Hershey, PA, 4
Higbe, Kirby, 150
Hockey, 32
Hodges, Gil, 279
Holke, Walter, 111
Holliday, Bug, 51
Hollmig, Stan, 226
Hornsby, Rogers, 252, 281
Hot Springs, AR, 4
Houston, 249
Houston Astros, 88, 97, 107, 135, 243, 257, 268, 311
Houston Colt 45s, 81, 85, 196
Hughes, Tommy, 124
Hulen, Bill, 109
Hulswitt, Rudy, 118, 173
Hurst, Don, 175, 192

Iburg, Ham, 154
Idaho Legislature, 20
Indiana, 63
International League, 28, 287
Inter-State League, 93
Irvin, Monte, 98
Ithaca College, 28

Jackson, Larry, 20, 295, 301
Jarry Park, 183
Javery, Al, 161
Jenkins, Ferguson, 107
Jennings, Hughie, 163
Johnson, Alex, 85
Johnson, Darrell, 163
Johnson, Davy, 293
Johnson, Deron, 7, 85, 244
Johnson, Walter, 277
Jones, Nippy, 29
Jones, Sheldon, 287
Jones, Willie, 67, 75, 151, 215, 259, 283
Jordan, Baxter, 125
Jordan, Niles, 231

Kaat, Jim, 181, 190
Kampouris, Alex, 29, 284
Kansas City Athletics, 77
Kansas City Royals, 84, 97, 113, 115, 120, 151, 172, 200, 237, 259, 265, 268
Keefe, Tim, 224
Kelleher, Hal, 210
Kenner, Harry, 154
Kentucky Legislature, 20
Kerksieck, Wayne, 29
Killefer, Bill, 115
Klaus, Bobby, 85
Klein, Chuck, 6, 15, 40, 58, 64, 67, 69, 92, 103, 136, 152, 166, 175, 189, 223, 224, 230, 238, 252, 254, 256, 261, 282, 285
Klem, Bill, 216
Knight, Jack, 46
Knowles, Darold, 91
Konstanty, Jim, 138, 155, 269
Koonce, Cal, 107
Koufax, Sandy, 114, 248
Koy, Ernie, 48
Kuenn, Harvey, 163

Lafata, Joe, 233
Lajoie, Nap, 223
Lancaster, PA, 240
Landis, Kenesaw M., 162, 271
Lapihuska, Andy, 154
Lavan, Doc, 281
Lee, Cliff, 111
Leesburg, FL, 4
Lerch, Randy, 46
Lerian, Walter, 94
Lersch, Barry, 245
Littell, Mark, 311
Litwhiler, Danny, 54, 87
Live Wires, 3
Lobert, Hans, 45, 60
Lohrman, Bill, 29
Lonborg, Jim, 190
Long, Dale, 140
Lopata, Stan, 115
Los Angeles Coliseum, 56, 114, 204, 207, 306
Los Angeles Dodgers, 17, 68, 159, 183, 191, 204, 207, 208, 212, 243, 257, 306
Louisville, 262
Lowe, Bobby, 279
Lowrey, Peanuts, 154
Lucchesi, Frank, 60, 255
Luderus, Fred, 84, 116, 151, 182, 229, 251, 259, 265
Luzinski, Greg, 25, 237
Lynch, Thomas, 271
Lyons, Terry, 186

McBride, Bake, 84, 113, 151
McCarver, Tim, 177
McGraw, Bob, 37
McGraw, Tug, 133, 190
McHenry, Austin, 281
McInnis, Stuffy, 205
McKee, Rogers, 12
McQuillan, George, 26, 90, 112, 144, 235, 248, 249
Magee, Sherry, 45, 136, 139, 215, 238
Mahaffey, Art, 14, 76, 106, 108, 126, 187, 193
Maher, Tom, 186
Major-league records, 26, 29, 49, 67, 189, 194, 209, 273, 276, 281, 288, 293, 310
Malone, Pat, 249
Manning, John, 244
Maranville, Rabbit, 239
Marichal, Juan, 38, 301
Marion, Marty, 21
Mathewson, Christy, 61, 144
Mauch, Gene, 60, 74, 253
Mayer, Erskine, 86
Mays, Willie, 102, 279
Meadows, Lee, 18, 276, 281
Melton, Rube, 222
Merkle, Fred, 132
Meusel, Irish, 128
Meyer, Jack, 53
Meyer, Russ, 249
Miami Beach, FL, 4
Miller, Bob, 80, 158, 172, 264
Miller, Cyclone, 168
Miller, Dusty, 105
Miller, Russ, 206
Miller, Stu, 168
Milwaukee, 279
Milwaukee Braves, 35, 72, 80, 147, 191, 193, 201, 204, 260
Milwaukee County Stadium, 56, 191, 193, 204, 248
"Miracle Braves," 214
Mississippi Southern University, 186
Mitchell, Clarence, 24
Mitchell, Fred, 163
Money, Don, 122, 238
Montanez, Willie, 64
Monteagudo, Rene, 307
Montreal Expos, 47, 177, 183, 190, 208, 212, 245, 284
Moore, Balor, 11
Moore, Earl, 150, 257
Moore, Joe, 29
Moore, Johnny, 244
Moore, Terry, 60, 188
Moran, Pat, 163, 221, 272
Morehead, Seth, 53
Moreland, Keith, 237
Morrill, John, 89

Mueller, Emmett, 48
Mulcahy, Hugh, 222, 246, 263
Municipal Stadium (Cleveland), 25
Murray, Billy, 255
Murtaugh, Danny, 58, 163
Musial, Stan, 21, 311
Myatt, George, 60

National Basketball Association, 160
National Football League, 17
National League,
  Championship Series, 97, 243, 268
  Eastern Division title, 97, 268
  first game, 1
  first night game, 246
  first tie game, 262
  hits leader, 99
  pennant, 47, 52, 97, 106, 167, 268
  records, 27, 61, 102, 118, 121, 189, 191, 210, 252, 254, 256, 267, 277, 299, 309, 311
  Rookie of Year, 131
National League Park (Philadelphia), 157, 207, 231, 241
Neale, Greasy, 17
Neeman, Cal, 38, 242
New Braunfels, TX, 4
Newcombe, Don, 129, 268
New York, 249, 257, 258, 273
New York Giants, 5, 12, 29, 46, 67, 68, 79, 80, 98, 110, 132, 144, 162, 195, 197, 207, 233, 240, 248, 252, 271, 276, 284, 287, 291
New York Knicks, 186
New York Mets, 32, 36, 43, 76, 80, 85, 91, 119, 133, 144, 176, 178, 180, 183, 202, 212, 231, 253
New York State curfew law, 76, 202
New York Yankees, 28, 120, 151, 155, 163, 167, 172, 200, 259, 260, 265, 279, 300
Nichols, Kid, 224
Nicknames, 63, 132, 154, 240, 263
Niekro, Phil, 88
Night games, 55, 246
Norwood (MA) High School, 32
Nottebart, Don, 81

Oakland Athletics, 91, 163
Oana, Prince, 137
O'Connell, Jimmy, 162
O'Doul, Lefty, 30, 83, 103, 136, 156, 230, 238, 252, 256, 261
Oeschger, Joe, 33, 80, 197
Oklahoma City, 112
Olympic Stadium (Montreal), 47, 190, 208, 268, 284
O'Neill, Steve, 60, 188
Opening games, 49, 98, 144, 176, 216, 238, 257, 273, 274

Orth, Al, 63
Ott, Mel, 284
Outfielders, 17, 19, 49, 54, 87, 99, 103, 128, 133, 137, 143, 147, 186, 189, 207, 219, 230, 232, 234, 282, 287, 288, 295, 303
Owens, Jim, 107, 193
Owens, Paul, 60, 255, 260
Ozark, Danny, 60, 74, 255

Padgett, Ernie, 111
Pagliaroni, Jim, 42
Passeau, Claude, 5, 150
Pena, Roberto, 122
Pennsylvania Blue Laws, 312
Perkins, Cy, 272
Peterson, Kent, 75
Pezzullo, Pretzels, 154
Pfeffer, Jeff, 80
Philadelphia, 1, 262
Philadelphia Athletics, 1, 3, 5, 65, 71, 134, 146, 157, 214, 219, 235, 252, 266
Philadelphia Eagles, 17
Philadelphia Keystones, 82
Philadelphia National League club, 3
Philley, Dave, 307
Phillies
 basketball and, 160
 best month for, 95
 birthplace of, 219
 briefest career for, 186
 bribe and, 162
 brothers in, 213
 club records for, 2, 64, 67, 116, 303
 coaches of, 158, 272
 consecutive games for, 116
 earliest games of, 116
 fastest game for, 276
 first games for, 1, 169
 first, last games, 245
 first, last victories, 5
 first tie game for, 262
 football and, 62
 forfeited games for, 216, 233
 games behind for, 97
 general managers of, 260
 hockey and, 32
 home record of, 305
 important dates of, 311
 longest game for, 241
 losing streaks of, 72, 106, 191, 193
 managers of, 19, 28, 60, 74, 134, 163, 188, 205, 221, 255
 magic number of, 52
 military service and, 263
 most valuable players in, 44, 138, 269
 names of, 3, 73
 night games for, 55, 246
 oldest, 104, 188
 100 wins of, 142
 one-run games for, 120
 one-run victories for, 34
 1-0 games for, 289
 player-managers of, 205
 players used in, 235
 positions in, 99, 201
 postponed games for, 194
 presidents of, 271

 rookies in, 102, 131, 153, 232
 rules changes for, 253
 sale of, 13
 shut out of, 144
 surname of, 168
 trade of, 133
 triple plays for, 85, 111
 uniform numbers of, 123, 217
 value of, 13
 victories by day of week for, 312
 winning streaks by, 190, 208, 296
 worst month for, 96
 youngest, 12, 117, 188
Piersall, Jimmy, 180
Pinson, Vada, 85
Pitchers,
 complete games and, 50, 57, 80, 88, 243, 264
 consecutive games lost by, 206
 consecutive games won by, 88, 177, 212
 consecutive scoreless innings by, 90, 297
 debuts of, 124
 doubleheader shutout by, 76
 earned run average of, 76
 first major-league game by, 231
 first victory by, 127, 231
 glasses of, 18
 home runs by, 29, 31, 35, 135, 140, 165, 170, 180
 legislators and, 20
 losing, 106
 losses by, 57
 managers and, 57
 most games by, 57, 138, 269
 most hits by, 57
 most innings by, 33, 57
 most losses by, 57
 most runs by, 57, 210
 most scoreless innings by, 80
 most valuable, 138
 most wins by, 39, 57
 no-hit games by, 18, 46, 66, 81, 98, 119, 173, 242, 248
 oldest, 104
 one-hit games by, 38, 61
 1-0 games by, 7, 69
 perfect games by, 36
 prediction of, 14
 relief, 53, 59, 91, 138, 269, 290
 rookie, 131, 153
 runs by, 195, 291, 298
 shutouts by, 10, 26, 76, 80, 121, 153, 227, 231, 249, 257, 277, 292, 297
 spitball by, 24
 strikeouts by, 2, 53, 93, 114, 126, 150, 202, 308
 thirty-game winning, 22
 twenty-game losing, 78, 222, 304
 twenty-game winning, 71, 86, 108, 185
 two games one day by, 101, 129, 218

 walks by, 110
 wins by, 16, 37, 57, 112
 youngest, 12, 117
Pittsburgh, 249, 258
Pittsburgh Pirates, 18, 32, 46, 53, 97, 124, 125, 140, 148, 163, 166, 183, 191, 192, 201, 207, 235, 239, 246, 249, 275, 282, 283, 284, 285, 312
Playing rules, 253
Pollet, Howie, 287
Polo Grounds (New York), 12, 29, 46, 162, 180, 216, 240, 248, 276
Post, Wally, 56
Potter, James, 13
Power, Vic, 85
Providence Grays, 1, 292
Purcell, Blondie, 60

Quinn, Bob, 260
Quinn, Bob Jr., 260
Quinn, Jack, 260
Quinn, John, 260

Radatz, Dick, 25
Radbourn, Old Hoss, 1
Raffensberger, Ken, 75, 187, 222
Reach, Alfred J., 13, 132
Recreation Park (Philadelphia), 1
Redland Field (Cincinnati), 101, 203, 249
Reed, Ron, 160, 190
Reynolds, Ken, 206
Richie, Lew, 80
Richmond, VA, 4
Riddle, Elmer, 124
Ring, Jimmy, 39, 247, 281
Riverfront Stadium (Cincinnati), 46, 66, 250
Rixey, Eppa, 78, 101, 222, 223
Roberts, Robin, 22, 31, 35, 50, 57, 93, 98, 108, 123, 124, 135, 150, 158, 170, 172, 185, 193, 222, 223, 264, 274
Robertson, Dave, 284
Robinson, Frank, 85
Robison Field (St. Louis), 197, 297
Rogers, John I., 13, 132
Rojas, Cookie, 154, 201
Rookie, 48, 68, 102, 112, 131
Rose, Pete, 41, 99, 103, 116, 217, 310, 311
Roseboro, John, 159
Rose Bowl game, 17
Rowe, Schoolboy, 75, 161, 236
Rucker, Nap, 144
Ruth, Babe, 189, 198
Ruthven, Dick, 172
Ryan, Connie, 278
Ryan, Mike, 272
Ryan, Nolan, 311

St. Louis, 258
St. Louis Browns, 9, 252, 289
St. Louis Cardinals, 12, 18, 21, 24, 29, 43, 52, 59, 114, 121, 127, 156, 191, 194, 197, 209, 242, 252, 266, 287, 297, 298, 301, 311

St. Paul, NE, 73
St. Petersburg, FL, 4
Sand, Heinie, 162
Sandberg, Ryne, 122
San Diego Padres, 43, 183, 190, 208, 212, 275, 293
San Diego Stadium, 7
Sanford, Jack, 108, 131, 150
San Francisco, 279, 289
San Francisco Giants, 38, 46, 47, 52, 68, 102, 131, 163, 186, 191, 193, 201, 220, 234, 250, 289
Sanicki, Ed, 287
Santo, Ron, 42
Santorini, Al, 7
Savannah, GA, 4
Sawyer, Eddie, 28, 60, 188, 255, 272
Scarce, Mac, 133
Schmidt, Mike, 11, 25, 44, 56, 84, 92, 113, 151, 164, 166, 211, 217, 244, 265, 268, 279, 283, 286
Schneck, Dave, 133
Schoendienst, Red, 29
Schulte, Ham, 154
Scott, Jack, 101, 222
Seals Stadium (San Francisco), 56, 234
Seaton, Tom, 150, 257, 302
Seaver, Tom, 144, 178
Second basemen, 19, 99, 103, 278, 309
Seerey, Pat, 279
Seibold, Socks, 104
Seminick, Andy, 8, 75, 244, 259
Semproch, Ray, 274
Sewell, Rip, 287
Shamokin, PA, 240
Shantz, Bobby, 106, 181
Shea Stadium (New York), 7, 25, 36, 46, 76, 80, 85, 119, 202, 231
Shettsline, Bill, 60, 255
Shibe Park (Philadelphia), 5, 8, 12, 21, 124, 129, 157, 161, 172, 184, 231, 233, 246, 266, 270, 287, 300
Short, Chris, 80, 106, 108, 127, 169, 193, 202, 249, 257
Shortstops, 19, 77, 103, 109, 118, 122, 162, 203, 239, 265
Shutouts, 10, 26, 39, 76
Sievers, Roy, 266
Simmons, Al, 252
Simmons, Curt, 110, 140, 187, 294
Sisler, Dick, 9, 27, 167, 268
Sisler, George, 9, 252
Skinner, Bob, 60
Slaughter, Enos, 29
Smith, George, 222, 227
Smith, Jack, 281
Smith, Lonnie, 237
Smith, Mayo, 60
Sothern, Denny, 207, 215
Southern Pines, NC, 4
Spahn, Warren, 7
Sparks, Tully, 33

Speier, Chris, 284
Sportsman's Park (St. Louis), 29, 287
Spring training, 4, 174
Stack, Eddie, 231
Stallings, George, 60, 132
Stanceu, Charley, 300
Stanford University, 17
Starrette, Herm, 272
Staub, Rusty, 85
Stearns, John, 133
Steinhagen, Ruth, 228
Stengel, Casey, 163
Stock, Milt, 281
Stolen bases, 45, 58, 70, 130
Stuart, Dick, 159
Sullivan, Frank, 76, 193
Sullivan, Joe, 149
Sweetland, Les, 69, 154, 257

Taylor, Tony, 85, 242, 295
Terry, Bill, 252
Texas Christian University, 141
Texas Rangers, 163
Third basemen, 12, 19, 103, 164, 211, 215, 286
Thomas, Frank, 85
Thompson, Fresco, 261
Thompson, Hank, 98
Thompson, Sam, 149, 278
Three Rivers Stadium (Pittsburgh), 46, 97
Tierney, Cotton, 111
Titus, John, 207
Tobin, Jim, 66
Todd, Al, 203
Toronto, 28, 287
Torporcer, Specs, 281
Trenton, 93
Trillo, Manny, 113, 259, 309
Tri-State League, 240
Turner, Tuck, 149
Tyler, George, 33, 128
Tyson, Turkey, 154

Uniform numbers, 123
Union Association, 82
University of California, 17
University of Detroit, 158
University of Michigan, 62
University of Southern California, 178
University of South Florida, 158
Unser, Del, 43, 115, 133
Utica, 28

Valo, Elmer, 65, 219
Van Dusen, Fred, 186
Vance, Dazzy, 81
Veterans Stadium (Philadelphia), 5, 11, 43, 46, 88, 157, 183, 190, 208, 241, 245, 250, 290, 293, 309, 311
Vorhees, Cy, 144
Vukovich, George, 226
Vukovich, John, 226

Wagner, Honus, 285
Waitkus, Eddie, 21, 27, 151, 228
Walk, Bob, 172

Walker, Gee, 261
Walker, Harry, 136
Walker, Marty, 186
Walters, Bucky, 187, 222, 249
Waner, Lloyd, 83
Washington and Jefferson, 17
Washington, DC, 4
Washington Senators, 63, 109, 143, 277, 289
Watson, Mule, 33
Weiser, Bud, 226
Wenz, Fred, 217
Westerly, RI, 28
West Side Grounds (Chicago), 173, 279
Weyhing, Gus, 22
White, Bill, 7, 14, 253
Whitman, Dick, 115
Whitney, Jim, 89
Whitney, Pinky, 103, 164, 175, 261
Whitted, Possum, 100
Whiz Kids, 3
Wilber, Del, 244
Wilhelm, Kaiser, 60, 205, 221
Williams, Billy, 253
Williams, Cy, 23, 67, 141, 244, 267, 280, 282
Williams, Shift, 23, 141
Williams, Ted, 23
Willoughby, Claude, 37, 165, 249
Wilmington, DE, 4, 124
Wilmington farm club, 93
Wilmington, NC, 4
Wilson, Earl, 66
Wilson, Hack, 224
Wilson, Jimmie, 60, 148, 205
Wiltse, Hooks, 248
Wine, Bobby, 85, 122, 272
Winter Haven, FL, 4
Winters, Jesse, 195, 281
Wise, Rick, 18, 46, 66, 250
Worcester, MA, 3, 13, 89, 179
World Series,
 1915, 84, 100, 113, 120, 145, 151, 155, 182, 199, 214, 226, 229, 251, 259, 265
 1950, 120, 151, 155, 167, 172, 200, 226, 251, 259, 265
 1959, 17
 1973, 91
 1980, 84, 97, 113, 115, 117, 120, 133, 151, 200, 226, 237, 243, 251, 259, 265, 268, 275
Wright, Harry, 74, 174, 224
Wrightstone, Russ, 283
Wrigley Field (Chicago), 56, 147, 166, 187, 210, 242, 253, 279, 284

Yankee Stadium (New York), 25

Zimmer, Chief, 205